A basic instruction manual for the operation of the body parts of effective bosses, or...

# *The Anatomy and Physiology of Leadership*

(Plug in any word for leader that works for you, i.e., manager, administrator, big Kahoona, team captain, boss, head honcho, grand exalted poobah, etc.)

# *The Anatomy and Physiology of Leadership*

The Anatomy and Physiology of Leadership

Written by Alan V. Brunacini and Nick Brunacini

Designed and Desktop Published by:
    Uptown Graphics & Design
    Peoria, Arizona

ISBN 0-9747534-5-9

Copyright 2005 Across the Street Productions, Inc.

All rights reserved. No part of this publication may be reproduced or transmitted without permission in writing from the authors.

# The Anatomy and Physiology of Leadership

## Table of Contents

Introduction...................................*iv-viii*

Front End.........................................1-30

Brain............................................ 31-48

Eyes............................................ 49-60

Ears............................................ 61-74

Nose............................................ 75-86

Mouth.......................................... 87-104

Face............................................105-114

Hand...........................................115 126

Foot............................................ 127-138

Heart.......................................... 139-154

Body........................................... 155-168

Gut............................................. 169-180

Backbone................................. 181-192

Funny Bone............................. 193-204

# *The Anatomy and Physiology of Leadership*

## *Introduction*

Awhile back during a conference my department conducts every year, Change in the Fire Service, I was listening to one of our speakers. He was very smart, experienced, and was making a very thoughtful presentation. While I was listening and trying to absorb what he was saying, an unusual thought struck me. It jumped into my head that we routinely package up and present management material from the "middle." We talk a lot about the application of process, procedures, and projects to improve organizational effectiveness--this is a good thing.

What we skip over is any practical description or discussion about how we, as leaders (bosses), use our very personal capabilities to actually do these things. We talk about organizational vision and never teach how to use our eyes; we talk about how critical communications is to all aspects of effectiveness and never provide any coaching on how to use our ears and manage (and control) our blab valve. We love to go on and on about strategic planning and don't ever explain how leaders should physically and emotionally position themselves to create an effective strategic message and outcome.

Going back and starting at the most basic beginning requires we outline and present in simple, fundamental terms how bosses should understand and use their human capabilities to create a functional level of personal effectiveness. It occurred to me that a simple, effective way to do this is to connect personal performance to our various body parts. Our body parts are the very personal "tools" we use to perform virtually everything we do.

# *The Anatomy and Physiology of Leadership*

This caused me to start paying attention to how my own and other's body parts behaved and performed. I also have become a lot more aware (and observant) of how the person on the "receiving end" reacts to the body-part performance of the person on the "sending end"... lots of times, the sender is a boss and the receiver is a worker.

I began to jot down thoughts that jumped into my noodle, things I saw, heard, and read. All the notes ended up in this little bundle, which is organized with a section on each basic body part.

In the past, I have mostly written about fireground management and customer service, so this little doodle has been an interesting (and fun) adventure for me.

I have asked my firefighter (Deputy Chief) son, Nick, to write a story to go with each separate body part. His tales involve mostly fire fighting incidents he has experienced. The stories are funny, sad, and sometimes pretty gritty... because what firefighters routinely do and see is funny, sad, and sometimes pretty gritty. The stories are a lot more operational than purely managerial, but if we can somehow use our body parts to effectively command and control fast-moving, dangerous hazard-zone service in the street, and to somehow consistently survive those conditions, we can pretty well manage most other things that occur.

# The Anatomy and Physiology of Leadership

As usual, I enlisted Kathi Hilmes and Harold Pickering to convert a set of expanded notes into a book. Kathi has been my PFD pardner for the past twenty-five years. She is a huge help to me and is a major player in the team who gets their crazy old fire chief through the day. She is the commander of the grammar/punctuation/editing sector and is a talented electronic graphic artist. Thank heaven, she got an "A+" in English throughout her schooling to somehow balance my "C-."

To avoid the clumsiness of frequently referring to the boss, leader, IC, etc., as he or she throughout the text, the authors have taken literary license to replace "he or she" with "their" when referring to the boss, IC, and other non-gender specific subjects, and until a new generic pronoun without masculine or feminine connotations is devised, we will continue to use the plural pronoun with a singular subject (Kathi says we are not in agreement with indefinite-pronoun antecedents--so we have put this in to let you know that we did it on purpose).

Phoenix Firefighter-Paramedic Harold "Pooney" Pickering has again done his usual artistic magic to cause the written stuff to come to life. His amazing artistic ability and street experience create a graphic gift that makes words more understandable to read, and a lot more fun to look at.

Our old friend, Doug Forsman, has also done his usual excellent job of coordinating all the different pieces and parts that must be somehow shoved in one end so they can come out the other as a book. He combines being a fire chief (Greely, Colorado) with an excellent knowledge of publishing and production, and is always able to make the process fun. He has effectively connected with everybody and everything at just the right time. The Oklahoma State University-IFSTA team is always a huge help to us. It is truly a joy for us to deal with and hang out with Chris Neal, Janet

# *The Anatomy and Physiology of Leadership*

Maker, and Mike Weider. Their support and assistance simply make this adventure possible. It has been an honor for me to have been connected to Oklahoma State University, starting as a young Fire Protection student (class of 1960) to now lapsing into old age with them. OSU has been an important part of everything I have been able to do in my fire service career and I am eternally grateful for their kindness.

Many times when we find ourselves in the middle, it's difficult to go back to the beginning. For most of us, it is a useful exercise to make that trip back, not so much to start over as it is to revisit, review, and perhaps relearn better (based on what got us to the middle). We should do this so we can effectively progress past where we were before. Most of us, based on what we know now, would be a lot better fourth graders than we were when we were ten years old. Sometimes, the best way to do the complicated stuff better is to get a booster shot of the simple stuff... we hope this material can provide such a booster shot that is both entertaining and helpful.

AVB, RNB
2005

*The Anatomy and Physiology of Leadership*

# *The Anatomy and Physiology of Leadership*

## Front End

# The Anatomy and Physiology of Leadership

*Front End*

# The Anatomy and Physiology of Leadership

## Front End

It becomes a major challenge to somehow sort out all the self-help stuff that is currently available in the ongoing search for the leadership development "needle in the haystack" of how to prosper and survive as a modern boss. Anyone who strolls through their local bookstore and looks into the business/management section is quickly bombarded by leadership "how to/self improvement" titles ranging (literally) from Attila to Zen (A to Z)--understanding and dealing with the techniques presented in this avalanche of material becomes an important (and fairly standard) part of becoming an effective leader. An organizational behavior pundit recently noted that if you entered "leadership" as an electronic search title, you would receive more than a half million(!) hits... that's an unbelievable amount of written blab about the fairly straight forward challenge of somehow lining up leaders ahead of followers and then getting the procession to go to some happy and productive place.

This simple little essay attempts to fit into the "front end" of all the lessons, directions, and advice in this A to Z development material by creating a personal framework to improve the engagement and effectiveness of the basic human tools we use in the leadership-boss process. Looking at leadership effectiveness from the very personal standpoint of our basic anatomy and physiology (A & P) will probably be a little different approach for most boss-behavior students.

This little adventure into body-part management is very simple and basic, and does not require that we mesmerize ourselves into some special trance to better understand how our basic human parts affect being a good boss. The effective use of our A & P should easily support and integrate with all the A to Z management

# The Anatomy and Physiology of Leadership

## Front End (cont.)

development stuff. While mastery always requires study, practice, application and refinement, the basic body-part rules of engagement are instantly doable because they directly relate to the effective operation of the basic equipment we personally possess, control, and continually pack around with us as humans... our basic body parts. We are in the very best position to self coach ourselves by learning, internalizing, and practicing personal improvement lessons. Simply, we are the custodians of how our body parts operate. No one or no other thing will cause those parts to change until and unless we want them to change... we are not going to change until *we* want to change. Good bosses become role models when they use (and improve) their body parts to create the feelings in the workers to improve the use of their own body parts. This role-model based encouragement is the very best gift a boss can give a worker.

Most of us boss types are just regular, ordinary folks who pretty much spend their lives plodding along on their daily rounds. It seems we don't have much direct capability to influence or effect the enormous and seemingly unsolvable big-deal problems like global peace or world hunger (WOW!). Based on us being just a little speck of sand on the beach of life, it's fairly predictable that sometimes we can begin to feel sort of overwhelmed and helpless and ask ourselves, "What can I actually control myself?" The short and sweet answer is "myself." The only person, place or thing we really have any consistent and really effective control over is *ourselves*.

When we get up in the morning, we have the achievable and understandable (if we study) capability to actually control such personal things, such as what we say and how we say it, the basic way our brain works, how we look at things, listen to things, what we do with our hands, and where we let our feet take us. Along with this personal performance and behavior reality is that

# The Anatomy and Physiology of Leadership

## Front End (cont.)

the only doable beginning (and basis) for our ability to influence anybody or anything else is for us to somehow make sense out of, and then capture control of ourselves--to a very major extent, about the only way a boss can really affect anyone else is by how they (the boss) act themselves.

Functional bosses use their own effective body-part performance to encourage, support, and assist the workers in doing good work by creating a positive feeling (and then the action that emerges from that positive feeling) about the organization, the work they do, the boss, and most of all themselves (self perception/esteem)... probably the most effective way for a boss to "control" a worker is to create an environment and relationship where the worker "controls" themselves. Simply, a lot of external "control" is an illusion--people *pretty much* do what they want and good bosses *pretty much* encourage them to basically do the positive things that their moms *pretty much* already taught them to do (most days, most of us [bosses most of all] *pretty much* have their hands full trying to control their own body parts--much less anyone else's).*

Organizations are typically arranged like a wedding cake where every successive layer "outranks" the layer below it. The reason for this basic organizational design is so there are in-place bosses on the task (work) level, on the tactical (middle management) level, and on the strategic (executive) level. The bosses on all three levels are responsible for managing their assigned areas.

The task level does the actual work (the business of the business). The tactical level keeps everyone "connected," and the strategic level provides resources and direction. Organizational effectiveness occurs when the three levels are coordinated, integrated, and aligned.

\* *The authors challenged to drive their very literate editor slightly nuts by writing a very long sentence using the words "pretty much" four times.*

# The Anatomy and Physiology of Leadership

## Front End (cont.)

Everyone has a boss (including the bosses) so everyone is a worker... the bosses manage their workers and are subordinate to their own bosses. Based on this reality, everyone becomes an expert in really knowing their own boss, because they work directly under ("geometrically connected to") the person who has organizational and operational positional power over them and is responsible for them. The "geometric" relationship created by the existence of positional power (formal) and personal power (emotional) that the boss has over the worker creates a very primitive (and accurate) awareness and understanding the worker has of how their boss actually uses their A & P. Simply, being a worker on the "receiving end" creates a primitive level of understanding and awareness about the boss who is on the "sending end" that is absolutely special to that hierarchical relationship. We will never (really) know what a person will do to us (or for us) until and unless that person (boss) has power over us. A "little" person (worker) knows how a "big" person (boss) will treat them simply because the person who is "bigger" is in an organizationally superior position.

A consistent, accurate, and sad answer to the timeless question, "Why does that person mistreat, abuse, or take advantage of someone else?" is simply because "they can"--or "who is going to stop them?" Most primitive awareness is short, fast, and powerful--there aren't many natural disconnects in primitive-level stuff--this is the very basic (i.e., primitive) reason why the worker really understands the boss. If the relationship is good or bad, nice or nasty, positive or negative, the worker knows it pretty quickly.

Simply, there isn't much "running room" between the boss and the worker. Based on this closeness, it doesn't take long for the worker to develop an (sometimes painfully) accurate awareness of the personal profile of the person (boss) who has direct, everyday power over them. With good bosses that worker awareness can also reflect that the reverse is also happily true.

# The Anatomy and Physiology of Leadership

## Front End (cont.)

Bosses have the ability to create a positive, humane, inclusive, and functional everyday environment for workers and themselves. Many times, the difference is simply based on how bosses use their personal A & P when they interact with the workers.

In this little essay, the boss/worker connection is daily and direct. The A & P dynamics describe the boss who is down the hall, not the big boss who is across town or across the country. The behavior of the boss at the very top is a big deal to everyone in the organization, because a lot of positive and negative stuff starts (or doesn't start) at the top.

The material in this essay is directed and designed to describe how the very personal (body part) behavior of every boss (regardless of the level) affects, influences, and connects (everyday) to the workers, who report to and directly interact (i.e., live with) that boss. No boss, regardless of experience, status, or salary is immune from how their personal A & P affects those who directly report to them. So the same process also applies to how the big boss's A & P affects those with whom they interact everyday.

If you really want to find out about the personal (A & P) profile of the company president, don't ask someone who sees them every six months at the national sales meeting. Ask their secretary, who spends eight and a half hours everyday with the Mr./Ms. Big Boss. How that person uses their A & P 24/7/365 will determine more than *any* other single thing if they are the boss from heaven, or the boss from hell. Simply, no one else who is not directly on the receiving end of how that person uses their body parts actually knows the day-to-day heaven/hell details like the worker who comes in everyday and sez, "Good morning, boss."

*Front End*

# The Anatomy and Physiology of Leadership

## Front End (cont.)

It becomes a huge personal mistake for big bosses to believe that based on their lofty position, big salary, and breathtaking charisma that they can stop paying attention to (and hopefully improving) how their personal characteristics are "connecting" to those "below them" ("below them" in and of itself can be a sad perspective).

Those at the top cannot escape becoming role models for how bosses use their personal components. An old fire truck driver, describing a badge-heavy battalion chief, said it so well: "As a monkey climbs a tree, eventually he will show his ass"... the same goes for bosses (particularly big ones). That worker-level view can either be pretty or ugly... but every boss produces their own view-- simply, there is no way to KYA from how well the workers "looking up" can see how the boss actually operates (sorry bosses)... simply, you can fool the spectators, but you can't fool the players.

Bosses learning to use their personal capability more effectively does not involve any fancy footwork, or clever mind games designed to manipulate or fool the workers in some mysterious way. Any such manipulative plan will almost instantly set off the worker's "baloney" alarm; conversely, nothing sends a more positive and progressive message than a genuine, "quiet" improvement in the personal performance of your boss in the direct, day-to-day ways that continually affect the boss-worker relationship.

In spite of all the amazing and unbelievable technical, electronic, data storage, information packaging and retrieval, compressed time nanosecond news reporting, and changes in knowledge management that have occurred, are occurring, and will occur, an absolutely constant (timeless) reality is the consistent inventory of human body parts. In fact, it may well be that all the developments in electronic-based information exchange has reduced the

# *The Anatomy and Physiology of Leadership*

## *Front End (cont.)*

ability of humans to use a full range of all their basic body parts to more effectively relate to each other. Instead of walking down the hall (foot) and talking (mouth) to someone (face to face), we now send 'em an e-mail--if we try to call someone on the phone (to actually talk to them), we routinely listen to a recording... soon we may become "electronic humans" who are unable to interpersonally engage in up-close and human, nonelectronic interaction.

We all are (and historically always have been) issued pretty much the same standard inventory of physical and mental pieces and parts at the factory... every normal person has always started out life with the same inventory of such parts (not including a place to plug in a computer). What you got is what you got, and (news flash) you very probably will not be given any new or different parts during your lifetime.

These standard, basic body-part components become the basic tools we all use to get us through life--as we cruise through the process of living, these parts all evolve and develop in different and very individual ways. Simply, this human developmental process becomes a significant reason why we are all separate and different individuals, each with a separate and distinctly different personality. This personality profile (i.e., A & P characteristics) will ultimately produce a special set of strengths and weaknesses and will, more than any other factor, determine the personal effectiveness (or the opposite) of any boss.

We learn to use our basic capabilities (consciously and very unconsciously) as a function of initial and ongoing human development and socialization. We are born naked, wet, and

# The Anatomy and Physiology of Leadership

## Front End (cont.)

hungry--they slap us on the butt, and we immediately and automatically start using our A & P. Simply, there ain't no warm-up period. The A & P learning process becomes so instant, instinctive (actually unconscious), and natural that we generally don't think much about how the parts individually and collectively operate--refining their use generally is only incidental to some other very focused and special learning/development activity... such as learning to tie our shoes, ride a bike, drive a stick shift, play the trumpet, bake a cake, etc.

All human activities and outputs are in some way a function of using our A & P. So as leaders/bosses, this standard, human-component inventory (pieces & parts) is what we come in with (A & P start up) and is what we are going to go out with (A & P shutdown). These personal capabilities become the basic human

tools we will always use to be individually effective; in fact (in a certain way), they are really the only tools we have that have been issued to us as the very personal assets (and liabilities) with which to be effective/ineffective.

The normal approach we mostly take to leadership development and study generally centers around trying to learn the A to Z performance concepts and techniques. The standard A & P inventory is basically taken for granted and is not generally regarded as being the personal tool of leaders, even though all the basic leadership performance and behavior we learn must somehow use the A & P inventory to act out virtually every human action... a college transcript contains such courses as "finance" and "economics" (A to Z) not "eyes and ears" and "brain and gut" (A & P). After graduation, how the former student instinctively (as opposed to consciously) uses their A & P parts will regulate how well they perform the A to Z activities they learned in school.

# *The Anatomy and Physiology of Leadership*

## *Front End (cont.)*

While a full range of professional education, self help, coaching, school, thought, reflection, and training are absolutely critical in developing an effective level of leadership knowledge and ability, the result of this effort is necessarily acted out in some way using the basic inventory of human A & P components.

The A & P stuff in this little essay is not meant to be a substitute for any of the A to Z organizational/business basic educational and improvement messages and lessons. The A to Z material is directed toward the performance and action that creates accepted good management practice.

The fundamental reason for effective body part performance is so that we perform effectively. We don't attempt to improve our A & P for the sake of A & P--we do it so we can produce some positive outcome. It would be dysfunctional (i.e., dumb) to become "professional A & P students." A to Z mostly describes what managers/bosses/leaders do (and how they should do it) to actually be effective managers/bosses/leaders... those management activities are the organizational tactical functions like planning, directing, organizing, staffing, creating a mission/vision, human resource management, financial activities and other organizational stuff.

The idea of studying, understanding, and improving the ability to use our own A & P better should make everything we (boss, mate, parent, friend, citizen) do more effective, easier, more enjoyable, and less painful.

Simply, this A & P material attempts to provide a teeny glimpse (i.e., self-coaching foundation) into how we might personally behave to be better at all the roles we play and the things we do (like all the A to Z stuff). We should think of A & P as the "WD-40 of personal effectiveness"--

# The Anatomy and Physiology of Leadership

## Front End (cont.)

a little squirt makes everything we do as bosses run smoother and reduces/eliminates the "squeaks" caused by ineffective body-part performance. The A to Z stuff is the gears--making the A & P more effective is the lubricant--nothing happens until the gears move. Well-oiled gears are mostly the result of sound, simple mechanics, not fancy, complicated academics.

Students of leadership should utilize this personal A & P development process to understand that every leadership action involves and requires some human effort, and that very personal effort will be measured by how effectively we utilize our human capabilities and components (A & P). Understanding and being good at all the technical, complicated, academic, and sophisticated development and application stuff is absolutely essential for leaders to be effective, but necessarily that standard management practice occurs on the "other side" of the capability of the leader to use their basic body parts to deliver those capabilities.

Our body parts are the basic performance tools that we use to do the application parts of our job. Therefore, we are effective only to the extent that those tools (parts) work okay. This is what we mean by the "other side."

If we are having problems with a body part (mouth, brain, ear, etc.), it shows up most of the time as an application problem--simply, the body part is the front end. The application is the back end. This "other side" challenge is that the only way (and place) to actually fix the problem is where it's occurring, not where it "pops out."

A lot of lunchroom conversations among workers involve their everyday frustrations of dealing with such (A & P) things as a boss with poor listening skills, or who uses their brain when they should be using their heart. Very little of that lunch buzz

# The Anatomy and Physiology of Leadership

## Front End (cont.)

involves descriptions of how well the boss is doing the complicated (application) principles covered in their last statistics course or the details taught in the computer class they took in college.

Leaders simply cannot out perform how well their personal pieces and parts actually work. When we overhear workers say, "What Waldo (the boss) does is okay, but, my god, how he screws up the way he does it"... they are basically describing A & P performance problems.

We can become more effective leaders as we:

- outline and clearly identify basic A & P input/output characteristics

- understand how each A & P component input/output affects the leadership process

- observe and study effective/ineffective (strengths and weaknesses) A & P performance in ourselves and others

- learn the effective rules of engagement for A & P operation

- practice effective A & P outputs (rules of engagement); accept feedback (report card) to adjust and continually refine our basic, personal leadership approach

- consciously and continually attempt to maintain a personal openness to improve our A & P effectiveness, based on input we receive from everyone and everything.

# The Anatomy and Physiology of Leadership

## Front End (cont.)

The trick to effectively using the A & P leadership stuff is to approach it in the right context. This ain't "rocket surgery" (as the B-shifter said) and doesn't attempt in any way to try to explain why life is like it is (mainly because the authors don't have the faintest idea why life is like it is).

This little essay only attempts to present a simple set of guidelines for using your basic body parts in real-world leadership situations more effectively. Don't make any more (or any less) out of it than just that. It does not in any way try to be the great three-and-a-half-inch thick social-science textbook that explains all the complicated dynamics involved in why or how we are programmed at the factory and beyond--it only takes a very fundamental (actually primitive) short-version "Mechanics Illustrated" stab at looking at how we are equipped (a basic parts list) and how to effectively engage (a basic operator's manual) those parts with a particular focus on the boss/leadership process. It is only meant (... no more, no less) to be a simple, immediately understandable, individually doable, and refinable instruction manual for our body parts and how the way we use the rules of engagement for those parts can impact our personal effectiveness.

This A & P material is directed toward the individual who is reading it, simply because that person (the reader) is the only one who can directly and effectively control the behavior of their own body parts. Let's use a very simple example:

In a conversation, you have a very personal opinion that is much different from what the other person is saying (meaning and feeling) in the conversation. That other person is someone who is close to you--relative, mate, worker/boss, friend, etc. If you blab out your personal opinion, it will not add anything positive or productive to the conversation and will (in fact) disrupt the relationship in some way--your opinion-based blab will create a

# The Anatomy and Physiology of Leadership

## Front End (cont.)

nonproductive argument, hurt that person's feelings, piss them off, create a negative memory, etc.

But it is a huge temptation to express your brilliant opinion because saying it will feel so good... simply, saying it was personally developed by *me*. I thought it up myself and the opinion is so smart and correct that I am almost compelled to express it--my personal spotlight is blinking so brightly that every cell in my body is screaming, "Say it."

The functional A & P behavior (based on the negative consequences) is to simply *shut up*. You and only you can do that. You are in direct control of what you say and you can quickly process in your brain the effect of what you are about to say (before you say it) and then send a brain message to your mouth to stay closed.

This simple change in behavior (taking control of what we say) would remarkably reduce the number of sofa-sleeping husbands, emergency-room admissions, and us wandering around after we said something that felt really good when we blurted it out and now we are muttering: "What the hell caused me to say that?"

Be very careful of having any body part want to do something so much that it either skips or outperforms a standard brain review. Only the owner of the brain/mouth process can control whether those two body parts compete or cooperate with each other.

The father/son doodlers who produced this little manual have based it on their very personal observations and work experience (80+ years combined), not on a lot of scientific/academic stuff. We are basically street firefighters whose college attendance occurred mostly because the school smelled smoke and they called us, rather than the school enrolling us (based on their academic standards). What we do for a living is a lot more like hockey than ballet. We land just

# The Anatomy and Physiology of Leadership

## Front End (cont.)

about right on the smart/dumb scale. We are smart enough to record what we see and to somehow log the lessons that our road rash has taught us... we are also dumb enough that the material is simple, basic, and short (just over two-hundred pages). If we were psychologists, therapists, social scientists, or upper-division college instructors, we would be so smart and know so much that it would take 852 pages of complicated text to describe our thoughts and observations.

> **Note:**
>
> While we are very respectful of these professionals and admire their considerable capabilities, we have encountered organizations inhabited principally by them and they seem to have about the same body-part application difficulties, boss/worker challenges, and human interaction problems as every other organizational collection of humans... it seems that folks are folks, power is power, and egos eat brains no matter how well the players are academically trained and intellectually developed.

We also have been bosses for a long time (50+ years). We have and are trying everyday to learn, apply, and improve all the A to Z management practice lessons, and have made about every stupid A & P mistake possible. What we missed in the formal classroom (ballet), we got to live through in a place where they give you the test before you get the lesson (hockey)... these lessons, and the classroom (street) where they are given, seem to produce a lot of educational road rash on our body parts.

We have discovered that up-close and personal trauma can produce a lot of lessons. It also has a very long memory that will keep speaking to you, and you will just continue to accumulate scar tissue until you learn to listen and then get the lesson (big-time, body-part capability).

# *The Anatomy and Physiology of Leadership*

## *Front End (cont.)*

As we have already stated, this material only attempts to describe the functional behavior of our basic body parts. This behavior is (like functional things are) mostly an acted-out process. This A & P stuff describes only the *tactical* use of our body parts. Tactical means it is behavior that is acted out (i.e., applied) physically and can be mutually "experienced" by the players through the interaction of their body parts... A & P attempts to describe what happens on the outside by the physical action of our basic human components. Not all the complicated stuff that happens on the inside ends up being acted out on the outside.

There is another separate self-help section in the bookstore right across from the A to Z management area that has its very own 10,000 books on each separate intrinsic human aspect that somehow affects and influences that very personal exterior, physical behavior. As usual, we will summarize those 10,000 books that describe just some of those ("inside") aspects in less than ten words. Once again, our shameless summarization is not meant in any way to reduce the importance of these aspects, only to make note of them as they affect the A & P stuff... and to do it in a way that reflects the authors' lack of qualifications to describe these complicated concepts in any detail.

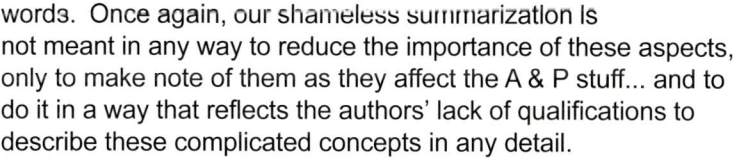

The following are examples of some basic stuff that describes the "human condition" that connects the A & P to the "inside/outside" process:

- power = use it (+); don't abuse it (-); to get more, give it away
- life = don't worry; be happy (it's basically just a big skit!)
- motivation = check your motives/if it's self serving, dump it

*Front End*

# The Anatomy and Physiology of Leadership

## Front End (cont.)

- soul = don't sell it
- ego = don't let it eat your brain
- emotions = manage the actions that your feelings produce
- getting old = not for sissies
- imagination = understand it--develop it--improve it
- ethics = do good/be honest
- ambition = be selfless, not selfish
- values = be nice (if you wonder, ask mom)
- happiness = they don't take it away--you give it away
- resiliency = cowboy up/don't whine (cowboy up = be tough)
- traits = load good/unload bad
- beliefs = smart, nice, happy beats dumb, mean, sad
- personality = strive to be better; behave so you like you
- rank = have others work with you, not for you
- status = don't let it go higher than your heart
- control = control yourself/don't screw with others (be a coach, not a cop)
- spirituality = help--don't hurt: you/them (= love)
- service = don't judge--serve
- love = be like your dog (unconditional)
- morality = do good/don't do bad--feel good
- character = mix of morality (feel) and motivation (do)
- manners = do what mom taught you.

These are some of the personal dynamics that are bouncing around madly inside of all of us that cause us to behave in a lot of ways. They are going every which way and can either be the

# The Anatomy and Physiology of Leadership

## Front End (cont.)

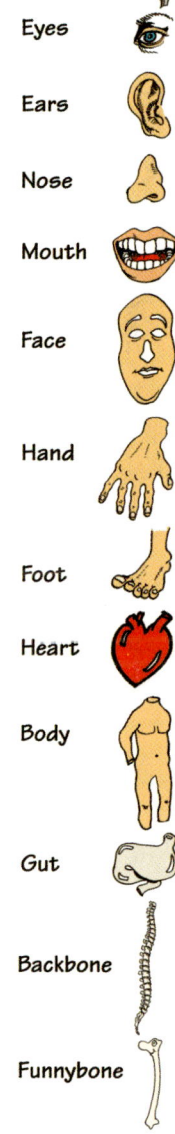

inputs or outputs that cause us to feel how we feel, do what we do, and they connect with our basic body parts. Those body parts include the following basic pieces and parts that each have their own special related capabilities (strengths/weaknesses):

- brain--think/remember/imagine
- eyes--see
- ears--hear
- nose--smell
- mouth--talk/taste
- face--expression
- hand--action
- foot--mobility
- heart--feel
- body--language
- gut--instinct
- backbone--fortitude
- funny bone--humor.

Serious students of leadership should not be distracted by the simplicity of the A & P Rules of Engagement (basic law of human enterprise: The simplest things are the most difficult to do well). The A & P rules become the very practical instruction manual for our original (permanent) personal equipment. Owners/operators (of any original equipment) should never take the instruction manual lightly. This is particularly important because our body is a dangerous piece of equipment... in this case, the A & P material describes how to hit the body-part's "start" button and then how to get all the components to somehow get going so they individually and collectively work effectively.

*Front End*

# The Anatomy and Physiology of Leadership

## Front End (cont.)

Sometimes things get messed up because we engage the original equipment before we read the complete instruction manual--it's a lot easier (and less painful) to first study the manual and then follow the instructions... simply, it's never smart to disregard the operating instructions that are in the owner's manual.

The fundamental rules of engagement (covered in this A & P manual) are absolutely critical to our personal effectiveness. Because they are so basic, habitual, and (potentially) so painfully personal, and because they impinge so directly, continuously, and with such a strong, ongoing influence particularly on the (power oriented) boss/worker relationship, the rules of engagement become not only the most important, but also the most unforgiving and difficult to understand and master because they are so personal and instinctive. Simply, in forty-five days, it's easier to technically reinvent and reengineer your part of the company you work for than to change something you have repeatedly done (habitually) personally for the past thirty-eight years.

A basic reality is that humans and the organization they work in quickly become highly integrated. How bosses and workers interact become a reflection (continuation) of the history, culture, custom, and style of their "company." A major part of that profile is how both the organization (collectively) and the humans (individually) use their basic body parts. That individual/organizational integration creates a close connection and eventually an interchangeability between the place and the people.

# The Anatomy and Physiology of Leadership

## Front End (cont.)

As humans become part of an organization and become assimilated, they necessarily react to the style of that organizational profile. Our four, basic, very personal options are: We can join, fight, give up, or quit. Necessarily, every individual controls their own personal reaction to these basic options. A major problem occurs when an individual quits (gives up) and stays.

Based on the close connection between the people and the organization, the only way to improve one is to improve the other. Simply, there are organizations that talk too much, don't listen well, are emotionally illiterate, and don't consistently stand up straight and tall and do the right thing. There are many organizations that happily do the positive opposite.

It's pretty easy to go to a two-day continuous improvement seminar (taught by someone five-hundred miles from home with a briefcase and a powerpoint), and to hold hands and sing, "We are the Earth." In spite of living through this thrilling experience, on most days it's really hard for leaders to go back to their day-to-day job and play their regular role and somehow change the entire organization all at once. It's also really hard for those same bosses to actually improve the performance of the people they directly supervise (it's a lot easier to temporarily move the workers than it is to permanently motivate them).

What if all at once, all the bosses quietly improved the basic performance of their own human capabilities just one percent. Yowee! We have just sailed past the moon!

If just paying attention as you read the human-performance instruction manual a couple of times and understanding and remembering the rules of engagement (a damn good start) was

# The Anatomy and Physiology of Leadership

## Front End (cont.)

all it took to get an A+ in Boss/Leader 101, most systems would work peachy and life would be simple. But life is not simple. A set of powerful, personal problems occur in the real world where another set of positive and negative dynamics continually bounce against all of our human pieces and parts.

These dynamics involve an ongoing struggle between a basic and primitive set of very personal angels (+) and another set of also very personal demons (-) that just naturally hang out inside and around each of us. The terms "angel" and "demon" are used only to attach familiar names to a smart/dumb functional effect on our body parts--simply, angels are sweet, smart, nice helpers who bring out the best in us; demons are ugly, cunning, deformed, stinky, sometimes evil little urchins who sabotage our effectiveness and cause us to do really dumb, ineffective stuff.

In this little essay, the names are used only metaphorically and are not meant to be applied in any religious or spiritual way. The reader can plug in any other names that work better for them... the authors struggled with eighty-seven other yahoo/ugghh, good/bad, nice/awful names and always came back to the easily defined and widely understood angel/demon ones (if you come up with a better set, please call collect). Words are weapons, and it is important for us to connect action-oriented language to critical personal effectiveness stuff, so we can quickly identify, understand, relate and effectively react at show time. A familiar, comfortable reference (angels/demons) also makes it easier (and more fun) to play the effective body-part game.

Using the rules of engagement to describe and to create more functional behaviors for each body part gives us a fighting chance to keep the angels that help our body parts running loose and to lock up the demons that screw up those same parts. The rules (of engagement) also create a very simple, understandable plan for our personal effectiveness. This rules-of-engagement

# The Anatomy and Physiology of Leadership

## Front End (cont.)

plan provides a very doable and rememberable launching pad for learning and performing more complicated and involved leadership (A to Z) techniques that should logically occur in the improved boss performance developmental process, beyond somehow coming to grips with (or even mastering) the A & P basic stuff.

These angel/devil characters don't just sit in the park, enjoy the fresh air, and then go take a nap--they are always (24/7/365) doing sets and reps (working out) on all of our A & P inventory. The ongoing score card for this struggle describes in measurable, objective, observable ways how well our various components actually perform.

The rules of this personal performance game describe what makes boss/leaders effective or not effective. It's really pretty simple... the body parts work when they join up with the angels and resist the demons--their performance breaks down when the demons sneak by or overpower (i.e., out tug) the angels and take over. The most critical part of this struggle is always going on inside each of us and the natural, ongoing process of competing with ourselves (angels vs. demons) becomes the price of admission to the "being a boss" game. All the sophisticated, complicated, fancy management and organizational development and application (A to Z) stuff occurs on the other side of this process.

In fact, for all this body-part performance commotion to be effective, it must result in some action-oriented outcome. The A & P improvement process is not some complicated academic drill. We can create the most effective A & P performance, but if it doesn't produce something tactically useful, it's just interesting (example: They don't pay us for having brains; they pay us for using them). Saying (again) that all the A to Z management stuff occurs on the other side of our A & P effectiveness doesn't in any way reduce how important the A to Z part is to individual and organizational success.

# The Anatomy and Physiology of Leadership

## Front End (cont.)

What this material is directed toward is that most of us skipped looking at our A & P profile on our way to trying to figure out all the A to Z mysteries. When we skip the A & P, we continually are at a disadvantage. We can learn the most modern, elegant management techniques, but the fancy stuff is just mumbo jumbo, if our basic body parts give up to negative demons and don't work effectively.

This occurs (as an example) when the system sends the boss off to the latest and greatest two-day whiz-bang management seminar conducted by some guy who came from a hundred miles away, wearing a color-coordinated suit. In most cases, Mr. Color Coordinated has some well-packaged, relevant information that is good stuff and does a professional job (generally in a sterile setting) delivering the material.

When the boss gets back, he uses two new four-syllable words that he learned at the seminar, and (as an example) continues to yell at the workers, closes his eyes whenever he opens his mouth, and suffers major grid lock on the hearing highway. In those cases, the workers say to themselves and each other, "Look, the system sent goofy, old Waldo off to another seminar." Waldo is a good guy, means well, and is trying to get better.

The major problem is that the system has never squared Waldo away on his (own) basic body-parts instruction manual, that gave him a fighting chance to join up with his angels and to body slam his demons. "Squaring Waldo away" means

# The Anatomy and Physiology of Leadership

## Front End (cont.)

providing him the standard inventory of body parts, describing what each part does, and then presenting him a simple, basic set of rules (of engagement) for each part.

Ideally, the system should also create a teaching, discussion, and application experience, in a safe coaching-oriented setting, where we can practice body-part performance to cause those lessons to "come to life" in a very practical manner. A huge challenge is for us to somehow receive focused feedback on our personal effectiveness, and then connect effective coaching to that input.

The vertical boss/worker relationship also complicates this process. It's pretty difficult for a worker to tell their boss that they talk when they should listen, and if they would open their eyes, they could see how the workers actually react based on how they feel. This little manual attempts to describe the body-part rules of engagement that we can learn, apply, and refine ourselves to be more effective.

In a very practical sense, the best chance we have at receiving effective coaching is for us to develop the ability to coach ourselves--this requires that we stand back from ourselves, examine how we behave (personally), and then apply a set of simple body-part performance rules (of engagement) to improve how we do/act in the next minute, meeting, or interaction. A lot of that coaching involves examining our very personal angels and demons-- improving how we help the angels, and understanding how we resist the demon influence.

Angels and demons are not simple, one-dimensional characters. They show up dressed in constantly changing costumes. Many times they wear disguises. They are highly adaptable, smart/dumb gremlins who come in lots of sizes and shapes. Always be aware that while the demons can produce a dumb, damaging, and

# The Anatomy and Physiology of Leadership

## Front End (cont.)

disruptive effect, they are not at all dumb themselves. They are really smart, resourceful, cunning, calculating ugly little jerks with long memories and an incredible understanding of human nature.

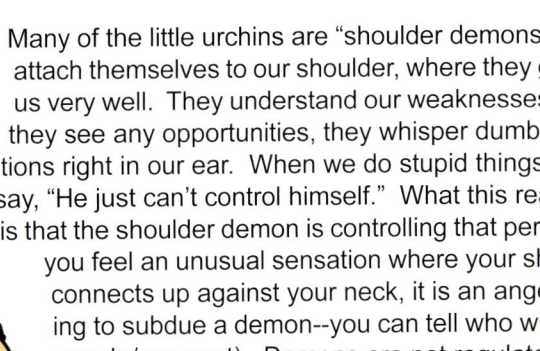

Many of the little urchins are "shoulder demons." They attach themselves to our shoulder, where they get to know us very well. They understand our weaknesses and when they see any opportunities, they whisper dumb instructions right in our ear. When we do stupid things, people say, "He just can't control himself." What this really means is that the shoulder demon is controlling that person (when you feel an unusual sensation where your shoulder connects up against your neck, it is an angel attempting to subdue a demon--you can tell who wins by what you do/say next). Demons are not regulated by any rules--their only objective is to screw up body-part effectiveness, however they can.

A real simple way to describe and understand what both the angels and demons can do is to consider them having an effective/ineffective, smart/dumb, happy/sad, nice/mean effect that can be small, medium, or large. This flexibility gives them the capability to quickly operate up and down an exciting, dynamic scale of intensity--what demons can do ranges from mischievous to monstrous/angels from mildly positive to astronomically altruistic. Both angels and demons always appear and operate in different (smart/dumb) very special personal combinations and at various levels (small, medium, and large), based on the body part(s) they inhabit at that moment, the details of the current situation, and the mood they are in, based on what they had for breakfast that day.

# The Anatomy and Physiology of Leadership

## Front End (cont.)

Demons have the very sophisticated (and devious) ability to turn around a very positive angel-induced characteristic--this is where a strength becomes a weakness.

Dealing with the angels and demons is never simple or easy (in fact, be very careful when it is very easy... the demons may be setting you up for a sucker punch). The practical essence of effective leadership-boss performance involves using the basic body-part rules of engagement, along with maintaining an accurate, ongoing size up of the angel/demon roll call (who shows up and their mood). This angel/demon size up becomes the basis of the capability to offensively keep the angels alive and well, and what it takes to defensively get the negative little toads into the demon hoosegow, and then prevent a jail break.

While the job description for each character (angel/demon) is pretty standard, how they line up and operate is a highly individualized process for each person. The roll (and role) call line-up formation and plays these positive/negative characters carry out inside each of us becomes a big part of our boss/leader personality. Simply, each of us is blessed with our own angels and cursed with our own demons.

# The Anatomy and Physiology of Leadership

## Front End (cont.)

Each of our thirteen (13) basic body parts are continually bombarded by the following set (actually a short list) of simple, fairly self-explanatory characteristics (expressed in words your mom would use *on* you) that regulate the effectiveness of that body-part component (readers can add any other characters that bless/curse their lives):

| ANGELS | SMALL | MEDIUM | LARGE | DEMONS | SMALL | MEDIUM | LARGE |
|---|---|---|---|---|---|---|---|
| kind | | | | mean | | | |
| mellow | | | | mad | | | |
| credit donor | | | | credit hog | | | |
| capable | | | | inept | | | |
| happy | | | | sad | | | |
| smart | | | | dumb | | | |
| calm | | | | panic | | | |
| nice | | | | nasty | | | |
| active | | | | lazy | | | |
| strong | | | | weak | | | |
| starter | | | | staller | | | |
| bold | | | | timid | | | |
| sane | | | | insane | | | |
| humble | | | | ego nut | | | |
| rational | | | | irrational | | | |
| secure | | | | insecure | | | |
| OK control | | | | control nut | | | |
| forgiving | | | | vengeful | | | |
| honest | | | | dishonest | | | |
| trusting | | | | suspicious | | | |
| supporter | | | | rival | | | |
| open | | | | closed | | | |
| enabler | | | | controller | | | |
| stable | | | | unstable | | | |
| lifter | | | | leaner | | | |

# The Anatomy and Physiology of Leadership

## Front End (cont.)

Obviously, most bosses are fully grown folks who have used their A & P components and capabilities for some time (their whole lives). Based on that grown-up reality, this A & P (rules of engagement) improvement exercise is directed toward making very doable, quiet, little adjustments in our personal approach that can produce significant (possibly huge) improvements. Most bosses do not require a massive personality change to improve their personal effectiveness... in fact, such major changes are generally impossible to sustain in the long term and are traumatic and confusing to workers who wonder how big a jolt of electricity caused Waldo to show up with a new fuzzy do, gold chains, and someone else's personality.

The usefulness of looking at how the A & P inventory works can be a powerful tool that (like most powerful things) can cut both ways--everyday, ongoing boss dysfunctions (demons) get acted out in a way that is up close and personal between the boss and their workers. These dysfunctional habits can be a drop of water constantly bouncing off the worker's forehead; conversely, effective boss behaviors (angels) can become a blessing for the workers who get to hang out with such a functional leader. We all "carry" our A & P components with us from our first breath to our last gasp, and the body-part "rules of engagement" become a practical game plan for continually making those personal parts individually and collectively more effective.

The next section of this essay will present a brief, very basic overview of each body part along with the rules of engagement (the real "beef" of the A & P drill) for that particular body part. It's

# The Anatomy and Physiology of Leadership

## Front End (cont.)

pretty tough to learn how a system with a lot of parts works, without first understanding how all those components work by themselves.  While each part has its own special capability, those parts typically don't effectively operate by themselves... in fact, big-time problems generally occur when a body part temporarily divorces itself from the other parts, and goes off on its own.  A critical personal effectiveness challenge will always involve both understanding how each part effectively engages, and then being able to coordinate the parts together.

# The Anatomy and Physiology of Leadership

# Brain

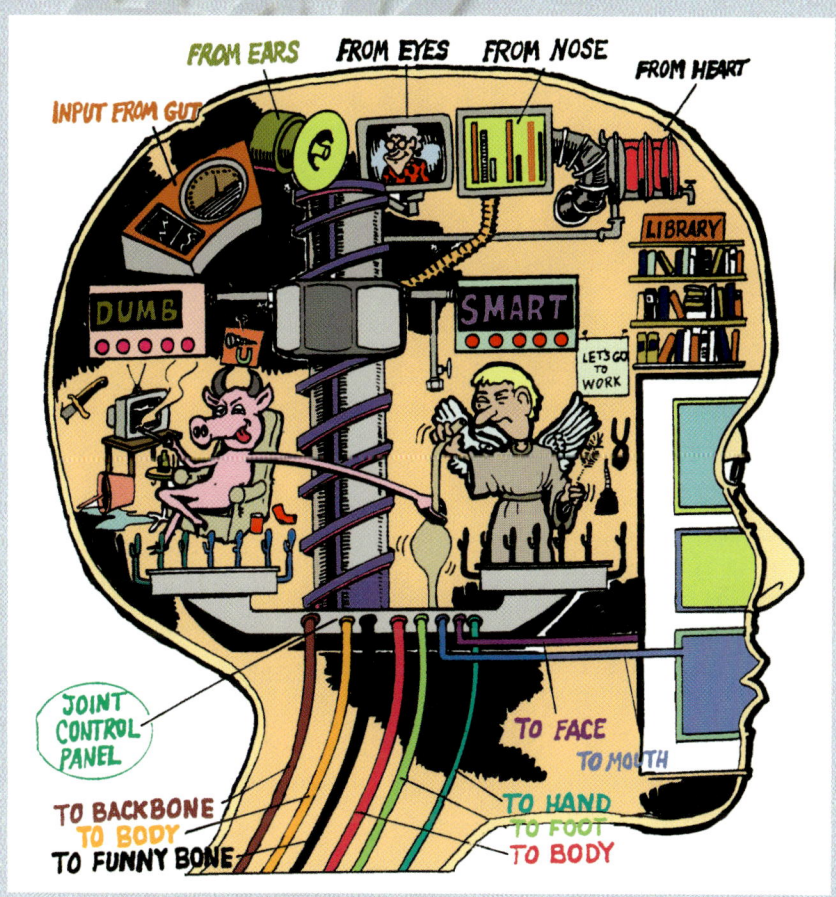

# *The Anatomy and Physiology of Leadership*

# *The Anatomy and Physiology of Leadership*

# Brain

## Basic Leadership Capability

The brain is what makes us smart/dumb and is a big-deal leadership component, because it is the processing place that coordinates, controls, connects, and mentally protects (... we hope) all the other body parts. The brain is the main cognitive control center for thinking, reasoning, rational processing, remembering, and decision making. The brain acts as "air traffic control" for the body by managing the inputs and outputs of the other basic A & P components.

All the other parts operate in a normal (and effective) way when they receive rational direction from the brain. The body part then picks up and sends intelligence/information back to the "control tower" (brain). This incoming information is then processed by the brain and translated into some kind of decision or reaction--the brain (like the control tower) then converts that decision into the mental orders and instructions required for other body parts to act out that decision.

When the two-way connection between the brain and the body part is clear (not blocked), the mental orders are automatically transmitted to that body part from the brain, which then carries out the order physically. Messages are then sent back to the brain from that body part (using the senses of that particular body part). That ongoing two-way process continues to make the ongoing adjustments that are required for effective body-part performance. This is where the mental and physical stuff actually connects.

This is why it is critical for us to both have "and use" our brains. The only function the brain performs is the rational stuff. While

# The Anatomy and Physiology of Leadership

## Brain (cont.)

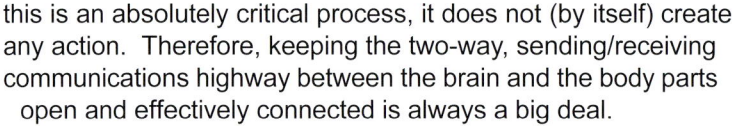

this is an absolutely critical process, it does not (by itself) create any action. Therefore, keeping the two-way, sending/receiving communications highway between the brain and the body parts open and effectively connected is always a big deal.

If the road to the brain is obstructed by roadblock demons, the brain cannot get the raw material (information input) to process. If the rotten little demon thugs disrupt the road out of the brain, there is no way to send "let's go to work" (smart/safe) signals from the brain out to the action parts. Blocking the brain is a common (and devastating) demon dirty trick. Another common demon dirty trick is diverting the message the brain is sending to the appropriate body part to another body part whose normal role is to do something that is not effective, smart, safe, or nice for that particular situation. Brain demons also can create roadblocks that cause the body part to independently act without first connecting with the brain.

Getting out ahead of the brain can cause that body part to skip the input, thought, reflect, and decide process. When there is this brain/body part disconnect, we many times default to nonthinking action. This can (and regularly does) produce dumb, damaging, and dysfunctional action.

Smart, functional players develop the habit of always engaging their brains before they act. This natural inclination is the result of living through the road rash that nonthinking action creates. This could be the most accurate (and simple) definition of "mature."

The brain is also the site of the personal storage library for past data. This library is where (and how) we store and remember stuff that has happened in the past. This library is also where our recall capability should always be running online doing a continuous search of the mental data storage, processing, and sending system.

# The Anatomy and Physiology of Leadership

## Brain (cont.)

As we go through life, we create "storage files" that become the very practical substance of what is called "experience" (or memory). How well we can access (i.e., remember), bring up, and use these "files" will, to a major extent, regulate how we use our experience to make decisions and how well we send effective action messages to other body parts.

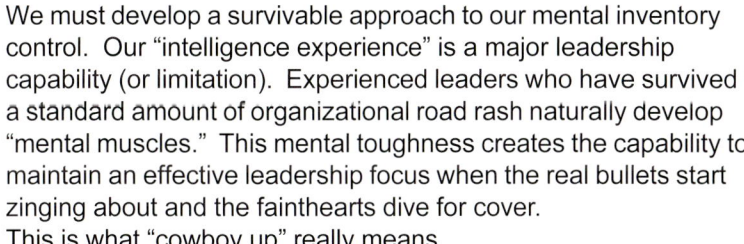

There is a natural limit to our brain storage warehouse. We must somehow develop the ability to unload the "mental clutter" that can stack up and make us nuts. Lots of seriously disoriented folks pushing overloaded shopping carts through our cities, talking to themselves, and hearing voices and noises no one else can hear are victims of this uncoding/unloading inability.

We must develop a survivable approach to our mental inventory control. Our "intelligence experience" is a major leadership capability (or limitation). Experienced leaders who have survived a standard amount of organizational road rash naturally develop "mental muscles." This mental toughness creates the capability to maintain an effective leadership focus when the real bullets start zinging about and the fainthearts dive for cover.
This is what "cowboy up" really means.

These mental muscles are also closely connected to the mental leadership temperature sensing and control system. This system can evaluate the temperature of the current environment outside the organization and create an operating temperature control capability that ranges from hot headed to cool headed. Smart leaders develop and refine the absolutely *big-deal* rational capability to remain cool headed as the outside temperature heats up.

# The Anatomy and Physiology of Leadership

## Brain (cont.)

- Access and use positive, effective experience/memory/instinct brain capability to identify standard patterns, to improve decisions, and to create smart outcomes.

- Develop mental muscles that make you a resilient, persistent survivor.

- Don't put stuff in your body that screws up your brain and can make you think/do very stupid stuff:

  - booze
  - drugs
  - chemicals
  - food (too many Snickers bars)

- Memory part of brain = personal "file cabinet"; select what to remember/what to forget:

  - File smart stuff.
  - Sort, remember, and file bad stuff.
  - Off-load stuff that makes you sad/nuts.
  - Understand that bad stuff "weighs" more than good stuff.

- Brain must always:

  - be engaged and processing
  - be in control of hand/foot/mouth--other body parts must consult with brain prior to engaging
  - always be gathering/filing/processing brain experience (experience = intelligence)

# The Anatomy and Physiology of Leadership

## Brain (cont.)

- engage smart side before mouth starts
- start mouth slowly
- know its limitations
- realize it's the only body part that can be mentally ill
- always default to kindness.

■ Continually use the shades of the gray color chart to develop flexible responses that match changing reality. Excessive rigidity can be the "kiss of death" in many management situations. Understand that some human activity must be black and white, and always operate only within these two colors: Simply, don't lie, cheat, or steal.

■ Try to keep your brain in an effective command position (engaged--open for business); check your thoughts/perceptions for accuracy/rationality in each situation or encounter.

■ You must develop the ability to identify and operate along the flexible (shades) and ridged (B/W) scale; developing this ability requires brains, basic values, and street sense.

■ Use your brain in a linear way: "Lay out" how what you are about to say/do will fit into and affect what is next and next, etc.

# The Anatomy and Physiology of Leadership

## Brain (cont.)

**Note:**

We have limited the focus of this little essay to the effective operation of only the thirteen basic body parts. This approach simplifies and limits the scope of the material to the fundamental "mechanical" components that we use day to day to get us through life. There are a number of other dimensions of the human-effectiveness inventory that are involved in the human operation. One of those components is so critical to our effectiveness that it deserves a special note. This component is the *ego*.

Unbalanced, out of control, unhealthy egos cause a lot more personal, organizational, and relationship disorder, pain, and wreckage than any other dimension of humanness. The ego resides somewhere in the body and is continually bouncing around (i.e., bombarding) all the human body parts. Like most of our human parts, the ego resides somewhere along an effectiveness scale that ranges from healthy, functional, and under control, to the other (dysfunctional) end of the scale where egos are sick, unrealistic, and goofy. Simply, any body part that can become inflated (like the ego) when it is self stimulated(!) can cause either great pleasure or enormous disorder and anguish. When inflated in an unrealistic and self-flattering way, the ego convinces the person they are someone who they are not. As that person acts out that screwy, ego-inflated role, they lose realistic contact with others. When that person is in the role of a boss, they have power over their workers and can use the authority of their position to inflict great ego-based confusion on the day-to-day organizational good order. Simply, wacko-boss egos make workers nuts.

# The Anatomy and Physiology of Leadership

## Brain (cont.)

Through the years we have developed the simple little expression, "egos eat brains" so even though our ego has an impact on all our body parts, we have placed this note with the material on the brain (egos eat brains). Because of the powerful emotional impact of the ego, the punch line of all this ego stuff is that we must continually do a reality check on the mischievous little transmitter that is continually broadcasting the very personal messages that create our own self-perception. The goal of this under-control effort is to simply operate in a place on the ego scale that effectively relates to the person, place, and thing with which we are trying to connect.

# The Anatomy and Physiology of Leadership

# Brain

Of all of our body parts, it's our brains that make us who we are. Our brain tells all of our other body parts what to do. It also holds and catalogues the events and memories that are our life. The most powerful thing our brain does is shaping and dictating our outlook on life, ultimately producing our personality. We are all special and unique--just like the proverbial snowflake. This is the only way to explain why two people with similar backgrounds react completely differently to the same set of circumstances. It's in their brains. The differences between our brains provide the variety in life.

This is a swell situation when you feel like getting ice cream (lots of variety) but isn't a very effective (or safe) way to do business when you are fighting structure fires (or participating in any other team activity).

Structural fire fighting has been a part of society ever since people began building combustible structures. One would think that much of the population would have at least a vague understanding of the basic ingredients that go into an organized structural fire attack. This is not the case. In some instances fire fighting professionals will take goofy, counter-productive actions when engaging in structural fire fighting operations. I believe that there are several mitigating factors that cause human beings (both non-firefighters and firefighters) to disengage their higher reasoning when a building hosts an out-of-control blaze.

Benjamin Franklin once said something to the effect that, "Fire makes an excellent servant, but a horrible master." Fire is a force of nature, and as such, can never be completely harnessed by man. Because of this, fire will always maintain its ability to scare the living daylights out of us. How terrified we become depends mostly on our proximity to the hazard. Individuals who cohabit the same space as the fire will have their terror meters pegged out.

If you want to find someone with the smug satisfaction of having all of the answers to the mystery of combustion, they will generally be located in safe confines, outside the hazard area. I have patiently sat in staged fire apparatus, waiting to be assigned to the fire attack by the Incident Commander (IC) and been approached by members of the gathering crowd. Most of these prophets have been intoxicated on any number of mind-altering substances that have opened the doorways of their minds, giving them the answers to the riddles of combustion.

# The Anatomy and Physiology of Leadership

They ask, "Hey fireman, why are you just sitting here? Why don't go over there and put the fire out? The fire is over there you idiot." They always boo the loudest in the cheap seats.

The fire department's primary reason for responding to the scene of a structure fire is to protect and save any customers who are stuck inside the burning building. Physically saving these folks is what motivated most firefighters to join up in the first place. Rescuing people from burning buildings requires quick action and highly coordinated team work.

Effective and hard-hitting fire fighting operations involve the proper amounts of front-end training, tools, equipment and management. All the rescuers have highly developed brains and understand their role in the operation, but their efforts must be coordinated and managed.

Each fire attack shares many (if not all) of the same elements, but they must be applied according to specific factors for that particular building and fire. Everyone has a job. The IC must somehow put all of the pieces together and manage a standard response to get the job done, while making sure that all of the firefighters survive their work.

The first chief who shows up at the scene transfers command from the current IC (usually the first-arriving engine company officer who is generally commanding from the inside of a burning building).

The chief IC operates inside their vehicle because it is pretty tough (impossible actually) to manage an ongoing, escalating fire fight while running around inside a burning building.

When command is located inside a command vehicle, it becomes a strategic level of command--one brain coordinating the activities of many brains.

Nothing will screw up a fire attack any quicker than having a strategic-level IC leave the confines of the vehicle and disappear into the smoke (see the Foot). This is strictly frowned upon and is always the result of brain overload.

It takes a resilient person and strong system to chain the dogs of hysterical emotional response, remaining clinically focused on your role in the task at hand. The old saying, "Once you lose your head the next thing to go is your ass" has never been more correct as it applies to structural fire fighting.

*Brain*

## *The Anatomy and Physiology of Leadership*

# Brain

The problem is that strategic-position chiefs all grew up (and developed their professional brains) as action-oriented firefighters. All chiefs worth their gold badge earned their street credit as firefighters by engaging the fire in hand-to-hand combat.

It is a proven scientific fact that when your brain is flooded with stress, it will revert back to what feels good and right. Swift, definitive action in the hazard zone always feels better than locking yourself inside a vehicle and telling others what to do over the radio. It's pretty easy to write this down, but it is really tested in the street when you are the chief at three in the morning, and you're the first one to show up at an incident scene that looks like the movie set of "The Dawn of the Living Dead."

It was dark and cold. Maurice (Battalion Chief) was dreaming and comfy under the covers. The electronic click opened circuits that blasted over a thousand watts of bright white light and a squealing dispatch tone that fell way to the melodic voice of a female Alarm Room operator.

"Channel 2, two-and-one assignment (two engine companies and one ladder company) for a reported apartment fire at 26$^{th}$ Street and Virginia…"

Maurice crawled out of bed, quickly got dressed, and headed out of his office toward the apparatus bay. He was met in the hallway by his firefighter driver, Luke. They jumped into their shiny, fire-engine red 1974 Chevy Suburban and headed down the road.

While Luke drove, Maurice began filling out his tactical work sheet. He had just noted the two engine and ladder companies assigned to the incident. When looking into the general direction of the incident, he saw a red glow punching into a small column of black smoke. Two minutes later, Luke was backing their rig into the driveway of the house that sat across the street from the small former apartment complex.

The brain is more powerful than any super computer. It can take instant input from any of our other senses, process and cross reference it with past experience and knowledge, and quickly evaluate what has happened, forecast what will probably happen next, and formulate a plan to deal with the situation. This becomes even more amazing when one considers that Maurice and Luke's brains were in deep REM sleep a mere three minutes ago.

I will say it again, "The brain is more powerful than any computer." To do something as

# The Anatomy and Physiology of Leadership

nonchallenging and mundane as reading the e-mail on my computer at work takes every bit of fifteen minutes. That's only the time required to start the infernal machine, log into the network, and then log into the e-mail system. Seven clicks and three passwords later I am ready to filter through the fifty to sixty e-mails that fill my box up daily to find the two or three messages that are actually of value and worth reading. Our service is extraordinary when you consider that in the same time it takes the average middle-manager to go through their e-mail, Maurice and Luke would be in the final stages of wrapping up the hazard-zone portion of the incident operation.

Maurice's eyes were seeing various small fires spread out across an area which used to be eight connected, single-story, red brick apartments. The corner that was once the back and side wall of the northern most unit was all that remained of the structure. About 500-square feet of still-attached roof covering the corner was quickly being eaten by fire. The street was littered with broken furniture, clothing, children's toys, jagged glass, blown-apart kitchen appliances, and everything else one would expect to find when people's homes are touched by a force that moves matter from zero miles an hour to the speed of sound in less than a second.

The only things left standing in the mayhem were three toilets still attached to their perches on the south end of the blast zone.

The house that bordered the south side of the apartments had been blown several feet off of its foundation. It looked like a giant hand had picked the house up and simply moved it over a little bit. Other than its broken windows, the old house appeared undamaged. Twelve minutes from now, companies operating on the interior of the affected structure would report that all of the ceilings had been blown down, and they had discovered and freed a sleeping couple who had been trapped in their bed by large pieces of drywall and mountains of insulation.

From Maurice's front seat, it appeared that his vehicle possessed the only unbroken glass in a quarter-mile radius. Maurice was parked in a position where the burning corner blocked his view to the north.

Stunned neighbors were starting to come out of their homes when it occurred to both Maurice and Luke that they were the first ones on the scene. Maurice picked up the radio mic and gave an initial radio report, "Battalion 2 to Alarm… we are on the scene of a gas explosion in a medium-sized

*Brain*

# Brain

apartment building. The building has been leveled and we have numerous gas-fed fires burning. We are going to need the gas company ASAP and the balance of a 1st alarm medical. Battalion 2 will be Virginia Command."

In the span of about five seconds, both Maurice and Luke had figured out that the apartment building had blown up as the result of a natural gas leak. They formulated a plan where they would get the leaking gas shut off, check the exposed buildings on all sides of the exploded apartment building for damage, and evaluate the number and condition of injured occupants. At the top of their list was to coordinate treating the injured, knock down the burning corner that was threatening the exposures to the north, and the grizzly task of searching the rubble for bodies.

The chiefs were waiting for the Indians, who were still a couple minutes out, when someone began pounding on Maurice's window. He looked over and came face to face with a man who was naked from the waist up and had sheets of skin hanging off his body. The fire had reduced the hair on his head to dirty stubble. His eyes were swollen and red. His face looked like it had been launched into a wall at a high rate of speed.

Before Maurice's brain could fully process the blown-up man standing at his window, several more badly damaged victims joined their neighbor seeking help from the lone IC.

The emotional response would have been for Maurice and Luke to stop what they were doing (which wasn't much more than looking out of their windows in horror), get out of their command post, and begin caring for the injured patients. If Maurice had been driven by his heart instead of his brain and had jumped into the fray of patient treatment, the situation would have gone from terrible to whatever is the summation of terrible, times thirty-two uncommanded firefighters.

Maurice knew that in a matter of seconds a group of people, equipped to care for the injured and eliminate the incident hazard were going to begin showing up en masse.

These incident responders only needed one thing from Maurice--to use his brain to coordinate their work and manage the incident scene. Maurice's role at the scene of working incidents was to be command and not to act.

# The Anatomy and Physiology of Leadership

It is impossible to command when you are cradling the dying in your arms. When faced with the difficult situation of helping the wounded or doing his command job, he told Luke, "Get us out of here now."

The casual observer watching Maurice and Luke drive away from people needing immediate assistance may characterize it as cold, cruel, and a dereliction of duty. Nothing could be further from the truth, and that is why we don't have uninformed, casual observers create and manage the systems we use to deliver emergency services.

If Maurice had succumbed to the urge to open his door, he would have abandoned his strategic-directed responsibility to the injured, the people still in harm's way, and the firefighters who showed up to help them. Maurice's focus had to be on the entire incident scene. That wasn't possible when the most heartbreaking part of it was staring him in the eye.

A few seconds after the command pair fled, the legions of disaster (an armada of engine, ladder, and paramedic units) arrived at the scene. Maurice's brain quickly went to work assigning the work force the patient-care tasks at hand.

The fire department ended up treating and transporting twelve patients, in addition to securing the leaking gas, extinguishing the burning rubble, performing search and rescue in half a dozen buildings which were affected by the detonation of the doomed apartment building, and extinguishing the fire that had extended into the apartment building to the north.

All of this work was completed within thirty minutes from the initial 9-1-1 call. The only reason that it happened in a well-coordinated and highly-efficient manner is because Maurice was thinking with his brain and not his emotions.

# *The Anatomy and Physiology of Leadership*

*Brain*

## The Anatomy and Physiology of Leadership

# Eyes

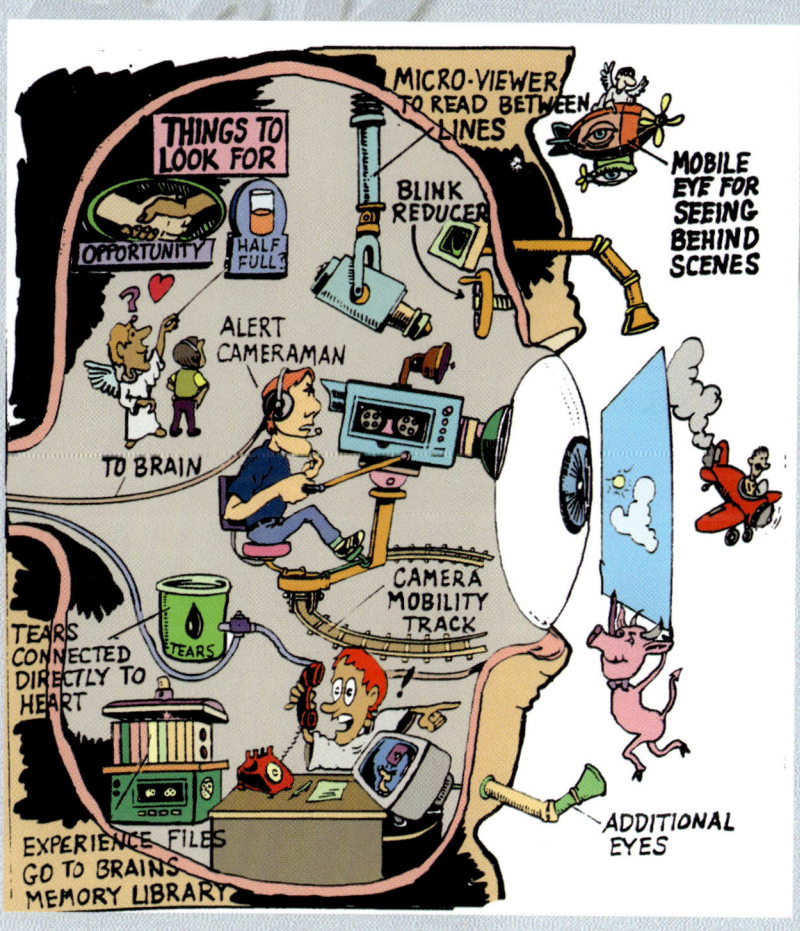

# The Anatomy and Physiology of Leadership

*Eyes*

# The Anatomy and Physiology of Leadership

## Basic Leadership Capability

Our eyes give us the capability to see, observe, and visualize. The eyes become a major, direct, and online way we optically evaluate conditions, action, and performance. The eyes become a major capability we use to connect with reality--the eyes have the capability to see what actually exists and what is visually occurring... we can read words, people, and situations. As we refine our sight (as a sense) we can also begin to better see what is "behind" reality (reality check point).

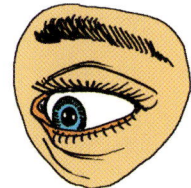

Effective leaders use their eyes to "look" where they speak/listen to continually evaluate how others are reacting ("social radar"). Effective leaders also use their eyes as a major way to establish personal contact with others. The capability of people to (simply) look at each other, as they converse, creates a nonverbal capability and connection between the communications participants--the eyes make face-to-face (eye-to-eye) contact the most effective form of nonverbal communication.

Where we physically direct our visual focus is a big deal and sends a major interpersonal message. We point our eyes to whom we want to send the message. Using eye contact, along with our facial expression, positive body language, and "friendly" speech (positive tone, supportive words, effective pace) becomes the commo package that effectively connects us to others. How leaders use this package provides an ongoing series of positive, interpersonal cues to encourage others to take an active, open, and ongoing part in exchanging information and feelings.

# The Anatomy and Physiology of Leadership

## Eyes (cont.)

Effective leaders also must develop the ability to continually use their feet to locate themselves in a position to visualize whatever is currently critical. This "visual mobility" becomes an absolutely essential part of the optics process and requires the leader to refine the commo connection between virtually all the other body parts/senses and the eye. All of those senses must send the feet a see with your feet "go look" mobility message, so they (the feet) can take the leader to the right place, at the right time, to be able to see the right thing.

Another major characteristic of the eyes is to distinguish various "colors." Effective leaders develop the ability to recognize and deal with a wide color spectrum (shades of gray). They work hard to prevent becoming "color blind" and are highly aware of the problems and lost opportunities that occur when they fail to recognize and effectively relate to new, changing, and sometimes unfamiliar "colors." This color clarity capability directly connects to being able to visually identify and deal with a highly diverse set of people, places, and things. Effective leaders train their eyes to both identify new sights and then to connect that visual recognition with brain support to positively connect to those new things. This becomes the foundation of understanding that many times being open to new things (sights) produces new opportunities.

### Rules of Engagement

- Maintain, sharpen, and never lose the ability to effectively focus--see both reality and meaning.

- Don't let anything hypnotize and tunnelize your vision/focus--stay visually agile.

# The Anatomy and Physiology of Leadership

## Eyes (cont.)

- Widen your view/look past "noise" (junk) for the "whole story"--look "deep" and be aware of what you don't see... always check out the "landscape" around the issue. Sometimes the most critical things are what we cannot see.

- Beware of anything or anybody that causes you to stop looking--be careful of "blinks"--never disconnect/ interrupt continuous looking.

- Develop the ability to know what to look at and what not to look at; only "look the other way" as a conscious, strategic process--take custody of your eyes.

- Personalize your communications with your eyes... you must be seen to be heard.

- Don't close your eyes when you open your mouth--be careful of your mouth (voice) seducing your eyes.

- Develop an effective understanding and balance between optics and perceptions; don't let old perceptions/judgements screw up new visual opportunities--perceptions should follow seeing (not the opposite).

- Wherever possible, get new/additional eyes to help you visually translate (then listen and look for yourself)... get help for whatever is new, unusual, and diverse.

*Eyes*

# The Anatomy and Physiology of Leadership

## Eyes (cont.)

- Look others in the eye(s) when you talk to them and when you listen to them... focus on the other person-- don't look down, around, or away.

- Eliminate distractions, barriers, interruptions, or anything that interferes with the personal visual connection you establish with your commo partner.

- Use your eyes (as a camera) to improve the information/ intelligence that you load into your memory/experience/ storage "files."

- Don't stop looking when you must verify what you thought you would see--look at and behind the whole scene-- visualize to see what is going to happen next (and next, and next).

- Develop and maintain an open and positive way of "looking at things"... particularly new things.

- DLR--doesn't look right.

- Develop the ability to:

  • Keep your eyes wide open.
  • Use your peripheral vision to see the edges.
  • Use your depth perception to look deep.
  • Read between the lines.
  • Know when to look away.
  • Look at the ugly/sad, and then move on.
  • Don't always believe everything you see.

# The Anatomy and Physiology of Leadership

## *Eyes (cont.)*

- Be careful of visual "sticker shock." Don't let surprising, shocking, unusual stuff cause you to stop looking... be visually tough.

- Don't let preconceived expectations, opinions, prejudices, or preferences create barriers for online visualization.

- Understand how powerful your eyes can be. For example, "rolling your eyes" is among the most disrespectful and disgusted messages you can send.

# The Anatomy and Physiology of Leadership

## Eyes

The truth be told, most of the information that our eyes transmit to our brain is the same stuff played over and over again. In many ways what we see is like watching the same movie every day. Such is the routine of life. Day in and day out, cab drivers navigate the same streets, heart surgeons perform the same operations on their patients, and mothers wake their children up, feeding them the same breakfast before sending them off to school.

People who lead lives with the potential for an expanded visual horizon are considered lucky. They get to see and do more than people who live a life of limited visual opportunities, much like the television commercial where the donut baker gets out of bed at dawn, half asleep, mumbling over and over again, "It's time to make the donuts."

Firefighters have a career that provides an almost unlimited potential for new visual input. Our work gives us a ticket to the carnival of life--its drama, comedy, triumph, tragedy, along with life's obscenities. We begin our careers intoxicated with the show, seeing things we hadn't even imagined, and watching ourselves do things we didn't know we were capable of doing. After awhile, we become seasoned and much of the mystery falls away, replaced by the routine. It is difficult to surprise, or impress, a veteran firefighter. Some days our job may seem repetitious, but it always holds the promise to be interrupted by an explosion of new visual imagery.

Engine 22's crew was on the way back to their station. They had just finished dropping off an ill diabetic at the hospital. The four-person crew was debating whether or not to stop at the corner taco shop and order some breakfast burros. Lunch was at least three hours away. The crew had already run four calls and they needed sustenance. It was unanimous, they all wanted chorizo and eggs wrapped in a tasty, flour tortilla.

Meanwhile in a nearby house, a lady had made a decision and it was final. She had worked out the details last night but up until this very moment, she really didn't think she could go through with it. She found serenity in accepting what she must do and felt a peace she hadn't known in her whole life. She finished the breakfast dishes and rounded the kids into the living room. Her two sons, ages twelve and eight, and her six-year old daughter sat on the sofa.

She told her children, "Kids, mommy has presents for all of you, but it is a surprise. You have to go out to the laundry room and close your eyes. Mommy will bring each of you your present, but you can't open your eyes or you will spoil the surprise."

# The Anatomy and Physiology of Leadership

The two younger kids were bursting with anticipation, the oldest child felt very uncomfortable about mommy's "surprise." For the last few years he had figured out that his mother was flat-ass crazy out of her mind.

It was Saturday morning and the old woman across the street decided to go out in her front yard to tend her roses. She had just finished cutting the spent flowers and stems back and was going to haul the trimmings to the trash when she noticed smoke coming from the backyard of the house across the street. She hadn't seen the neighbor kids all morning and the car wasn't in the driveway. Not knowing what else to do, she went inside and called 9-1-1.

Engine 22 had just put its turn signal on, letting the traffic behind it know that the crew was headed toward a gastronomical delight. At the same moment, millions of dollars worth of high-tech communications electronics triangulated its exact location (along with over one hundred other emergency response vehicles), determined it to be the closest appropriate unit and selected Engine 22 for the reported shed fire one block away.

Engine 22's captain heard the tone at the same time his mobile computer terminal beeped and lit up with the dispatch information. He said, "Life ain't fair boys. No chow for us. We just got popped for a shed fire."

The engineer groaned as he disengaged his turn signal and flipped his emergency lights and siren on. Breakfast would have to wait. Right now, none of them had any idea that they wouldn't feel like eating for quite some time.

The captain killed the siren as the engineer turned down the street leading into the quiet, old neighborhood. The engineer stopped in front of the small house. Seeing they had something burning behind the house and knowing that the captain and two firefighters would need a few minutes to get their protective gear (coat, helmet, and hood) on before fighting the fire, the engineer shifted his rig into pump gear, set the brake, and jumped out of the truck and pulled the attack line for his crew. While he was doing this, the two firefighters were hurriedly getting their turnouts on, while their captain sized up the situation and gave an initial-radio report.

He reported, "Engine 22 is on the scene of a small house. We have smoke showing from a carport laundry room that is connected to the house through a breezeway. We are pulling an inch and a half attack line for search, rescue, and fire control. We are operating in the offensive strategy. Engine 22 will be command. Give me the balance of a 2 and 1*."

\* 2 and 1 = 2 engine companies and 1 ladder company

# The Anatomy and Physiology of Leadership

The laundry room was located at the end of the driveway. A gate that led into the backyard separated the detached laundry room from the house. The captain's biggest concern was knocking down the little bit of fire in the laundry room and the rear of the house, and making sure that the fire didn't extend up into the common attic that the laundry room and carport shared with the house.

The engineer had just finished flaking out the 150 feet of attack line and went to the pump panel to charge the line with water. The senior firefighter was fully turned out, had just snapped his regulator into his SCBA face piece, and was now ready to do business. He grabbed the fog nozzle that was connected to end of the attack line, and cracked it open to bleed the air out of the line. The line hissed and spit a mixture of air and water for a few seconds, followed by a powerful stream of water.

The captain and second firefighter had finished donning their protective gear and were joining the senior firefighter. The engineer knew their next-due engine company was at least four or five minutes away, and his crew may use more than the 450 gallons that their truck carried in its water tank. He needed a close fire hydrant so he could hand jack (physically pull) a supply line.

The engineer had the hydrant valve and wrench in one hand and a piece of four-inch supply line in the other. He was walking the line back to a fire plug behind his truck when a twelve-year old boy stopped him. He could see that the kid had some minor burns on his hands and that he had been crying. He also had a story that couldn't wait for the hydrant hook up.

The captain and his two firefighters knocked down the fire in the small laundry room for the second time. The fire had been started with gasoline and kept reigniting. The firefighter opened the nozzle all of the way and was liberally applying water when the captain saw a small arm sticking out from under a pile of smoldering laundry. He reached down and pulled a badly burned little girl out of the mound of debris. He instantly knew she was dead.

The twelve-year old had led the engineer to the side of the house where he had stashed his little brother. The twelve-year old was crushed over the fact that he was only able to pull his little brother out of the burning room; but no matter how hard he tried, he couldn't get his sister out of the laundry room.

# The Anatomy and Physiology of Leadership

Between the heat of the fire and his possessed mother, he was severely overmatched. It was a miracle that he was able to pull his brother out before they both burned to death. His little brother was trying to tell the story surrounding the morning events to the engineer, but he had suffered serious burns to his airway and was having trouble speaking. The engineer listened, as the older brother filled in the missing pieces.

The engineer gathered the little boys at his rig, retrieved his captain and firefighter (both of them were paramedics) to treat the brothers. This left the senior firefighter to deal with the fire. The fire in the laundry room had extended beyond its ceiling, and now brown smoke was showing from the vents in the roof over the house. The firefighter pulled his line out of the laundry room/carport area and advanced it through the gate into the backyard. His plan was to knock down the fire that was burning somewhere behind the laundry room in the backyard and then move into the house from the back door.

He felt sad at the thought that the little girl had probably been playing with matches. He hated calls that involved kids because he had his own children, and no matter how hard he tried, he always saw the faces of his own offspring in these children. After he turned the corner into the backyard, he was forever cured from the curse of seeing his own children's faces in the dead.

He had walked through the gate, looked back to where he had just been, and pulled enough line to make the corner into the backyard. He turned to his left, towards the back of the laundry room and simply stared.

He couldn't make any sense of the information that his eyes were pumping into his brain. Fifteen feet away from him stood a burning adult.

The person was unaware of his presence and was dumping gasoline over their lower body. The person was bathed in flame.

The firefighter did the only thing he knew--he cracked the nozzle partially open and put the human being out. This alerted the burning effigy to his presence. The now smoldering person turned toward the firefighter. As it walked toward him, it raised the can of gas and doused its head, flame exploded twelve feet into the air, all the way to the peak of the roof.

Now it was difficult to distinguish the person in the center of the fireball. He stood in stunned visual disbelief as the free-burning human

# Eyes

continued to walk right at him. He opened the line again while taking a step back. This knocked down the fire and caused a repeated application of gas from the can with the same bonfire effect.

Now in serious doubt about his own safety, the firefighter opened the nozzle all of the way, applying all 125 gallons a minute that his line was capable of flowing. Between the volume and pressure the hose stream produced, the burning human was knocked to the ground and extinguished.

The suicidal human turned out to be the mother. Everyone involved with the incident couldn't believe their eyes (or any other of their body parts) that she was still alive. All of her hair had been consumed by the self-inflicted fire. One-hundred percent of her skin had the appearance of chocolate-colored, shrink-wrapped plastic. It is unknown by anyone why the woman didn't die immediately following her gasoline shampoo, how she made it to the hospital alive, and actually recovered from the event (if you can call living in agonizing physical pain for the rest of your life a recovery). Perhaps some greater power arranged her survival, as payment for setting her own children on fire. There are not answers to everything we see.

# The Anatomy and Physiology of Leadership

## Ears

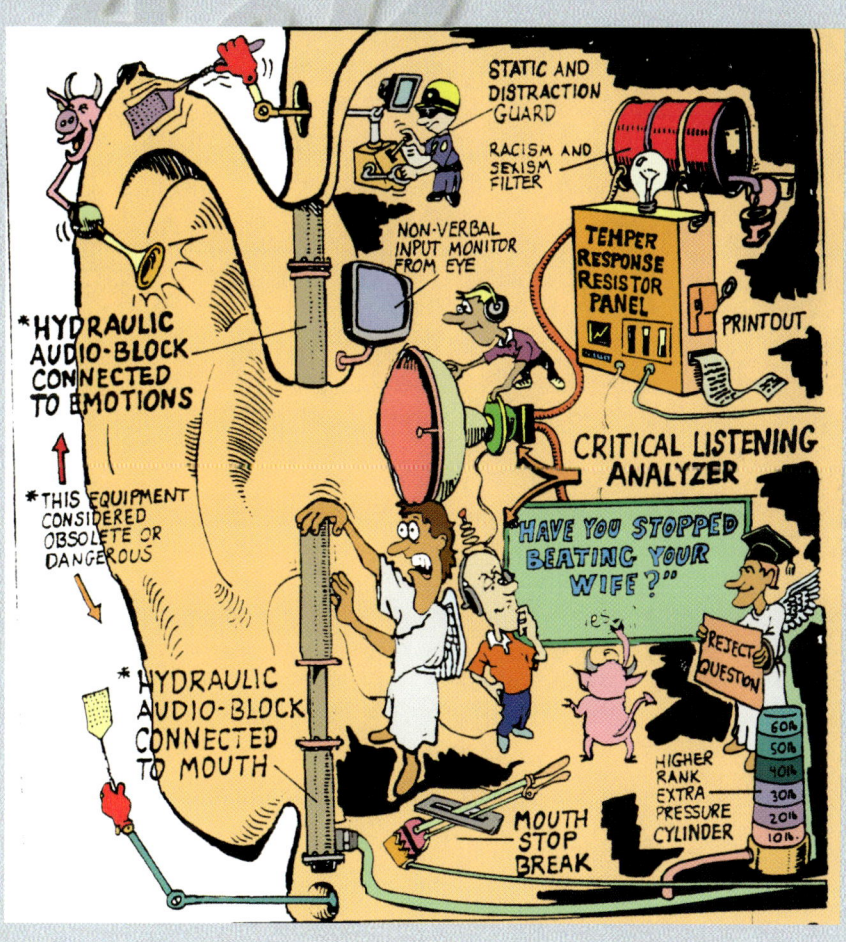

# The Anatomy and Physiology of Leadership

*Ears*

# The Anatomy and Physiology of Leadership

# Ears

## Basic Leadership Capability

Our ability to effectively listen provides a major form of information gathering and input. Such input becomes a critical source of the informational raw material that is transmitted from the ear to the brain for data processing and learning. The ability and willingness to critically listen also sends a strong, positive interpersonal message that the leader cares and feels that what others say (both verbally and nonverbally) is important to them. The inclination to consistently listen, pay attention, and then react to what is said becomes a major source of leadership credibility and trust. Every leader develops their own listening style and reputation (whether they want it or not) and how leaders listen/or don't listen becomes a major element in how that leader fits into organizational life.

Effective leaders use a combination of their body parts to develop a versatlle approach to different listening situations. The characteristics and intensity of each particular listening incident requires different "sized" ears--sometimes the leader puts on "big" ears, turns up the hearing dials, and does high-performance listening. Other less intensive situations require the controls to be turned down a bit and the boss uses a more relaxed hearing approach ("smaller" ears). Some situations produce toxic, damaging sounds where effective ear managers must use personal hearing protection (physical and psychological) to prevent permanent hearing loss.

Being able to match the ear size to the situation eliminates listening overload, and then burn out. It increases leadership effectiveness, endurance, and personal sanity. Engaged, active, and responsive listening shows up on every list (along with patience) that workers construct to describe effective bosses. On every list customers construct what describes responsive,

*Ears*

# The Anatomy and Physiology of Leadership

## Ears (cont.)

continuously connected service providers. This identified importance means listening is high-value, interpersonal action to those who are on the talking end of the communications process. Those who manage the upward mobility system must be very aware (and careful) of the serious problem created when promotion negatively affects hearing (higher rank sometimes impairs hearing).

Effective leaders must develop the resiliency to hear about things that are unpleasant, negative, sad, confusing, and disappointing. This "tough listening" capability requires the boss to transmit an authentic message that it is okay to send bad news if things are actually bad, and that the most serious problems occur when we fail to do just that. Over time, the workers will find out if it's really okay to deliver lousy news, based on how the boss actually listens, and then how the boss reacts.

Simply, the best way to see if empowerment to actually engage tough issues is beef or baloney is to do some empowered thing and then to see what happens. The point of the listening process is that it produces some related response. The action the boss takes after they listen becomes an integrated and critical part of the listening process, because that reaction will cause the workers to either keep communicating or start hiding out.

### Rules of Engagement

- Lots of reactions compete with listening--realize that your own blabbing/anger/emotion/ego conflicts with effective hearing--control your own hearing distractions and emotions.

- Continually sort out and block "static" (i.e., obstacles, barriers) to clear the way for effective hearing.

# The Anatomy and Physiology of Leadership

## Ears (cont.)

- Listen patiently: hear the whole message--listen critically (past the sound) for emotion/feeling/meaning.

- Realize that listening is (a lot) more difficult and less fun than talking.

- Use your mouth/eyes/face/body to encourage others to talk--this creates hearing opportunities (opportunities = ask/shut up/listen/react).

- Listen past what is said for what is *not* said.

- DSR--doesn't sound right.

- Pay attention--make eye contact (listen with your eyes) when you listen.

- Be careful of becoming tone deaf for certain sounds (opinion, prejudice, perception, tuned out, turned off, etc.).

- Try to listen your way out of tough spots instead of talking your way out.

- Lots of times workers will interrupt what the boss is doing with, "Have you got a minute?" and the boss must:

  - stop what they are doing
  - move from behind the desk to the "listening table"
  - shut off phones
  - close the door
  - be patient--focus (engaged eye contact) on the other person
  - listen and react.

*Ears*

# The Anatomy and Physiology of Leadership

## Ears (cont.)

- Realize that listening is fragile--don't let other body parts cut off hearing... hold/delay your perception/judgement/opinion/preference while you listen.

- Connect your ears to your brain *ahead* of your mouth--be careful of saying stuff that has not been entered, processed, and "cleared" by the brain.

- Don't turn off talkers--give continual interpersonal feedback that sends positive, encouraging messages that your ears are open for business:

  - Pay attention.
  - Don't judge... listen.
  - Get comfortable with silence.
  - Eliminate distractions.
  - Don't interrupt/abruptly change subject.
  - Use voice, face, and body to send "let's communicate" message.
  - Ask questions (open ended) to create talking/listening opportunities.
  - Don't jump to the solution... shut up and listen to the whole message.
  - Learn to "squint" with your ears.

- Time your listening to match the pace and approach of the talker--generally you can "listen" (and think) faster than they can talk--stay with them. Don't jump ahead; don't abruptly change the subject. Look for cues to respond effectively. Stay "connected" to the talker.

# The Anatomy and Physiology of Leadership

## Ears (cont.)

- Use big ears/little ears, based on each particular situation.

- Be careful not to base a reaction on the first version of a story that someone tells you; take time to get the whole story... avoid the "ready-fire-aim" approach to reacting to what you hear.

- Be careful of communication filters that restrict your capability to effectively listen, process, and react:

  - age
  - gender
  - race
  - ego
  - resentment
  - anger
  - mistrust.

- For clarification, use the "Columbo" approach: "I'm a little unclear, can you tell me more about..."; "I want to be sure I'm understanding what you're saying"; "Would you go over that again?"

- Be careful of what you say... particularly around those who you think are unconscious--hearing is the last sense to go.

- The best way to get someone else to listen to you is to listen to them.

- You generally don't learn much when your lips are moving.

# The Anatomy and Physiology of Leadership

## Ears

We are a visual species. The things we see oftentimes overpower what we hear. One picture is worth a thousand words. I am not demeaning our ears in favor of our sight. The people who make expensive Hollywood movies feel that the audio track of a film is every bit as important as what you see on the screen. What scares us the most is stuff we can't see-- the things that go bump in the night. One of the keys to life is to balance what we see with what we hear.

Our ears are wonderful devices that are always on and take no effort at all to operate. Verbal language is still the quickest and most powerful way that we have to communicate with one another. If you find yourself in a land where your ears don't comprehend the language, it's pretty tough to order off the menu. The problem that afflicts some people is that they have trouble listening. It's not that their ears don't work. They simply place a much higher premium on what they have to say and think; what other people have to say takes a distant second.

There are other times when we don't react according to what our ears and eyes are telling us. Our brain believes what it wants to believe and it will not be convinced otherwise. Some people refer to the high end of this spectrum as "shock." When we undergo some type of heavy emotional event it takes a while for our brain to sort out what the other senses transmitted.

The other slower end of the scale is what daily life does to us. Everyday we process lots of information, much of it delivered by our ears. Over the course of time we come to believe a certain set of values and beliefs because our external world and the people around us tell us they are true. We become very comfortable with the way things are. This is why it is so hard to change.

When I was hired as a firefighter, I joined an organization that had a lot of old-timers. Some of these men fought during the Second World War. They had a very strong sense of who they were and how things should be.

The reality of the time was that our service was undergoing massive change. During the late seventies and early eighties, fire departments all across the country were changing, not only the business that they did, but how they did it.

The all-male closed societies of the American fire service were hiring women. If that wasn't bad enough, we were also adding emergency medical response to our service delivery menu.

Many of these early pioneers stood in the center of the tracks and refused to listen to what their ears were telling them. The train of

# The Anatomy and Physiology of Leadership

change never slowed down, as it accelerated right over the top of them. Most of these guys were gone within a few years.

In the old days, the new guys had to carry their share of the water before they were completely accepted. It was a slow and painful process, taking years before you were considered an equal.

The new system did not worship at the same altar. Now a firefighter with a mere year of experience could become a paramedic. Medical calls quickly outpaced fire calls by four to one. This created a system where the younger members of the organization (paramedics) took control of most of the calls to which the fire department responded.

Older captains would loiter in the background and listen in amazement, not believing their ears, as two-year paramedic firefighters talked into a phone carried in a portable orange box (in the ancient pre-cell phone days) and said words like, "trigemini, traumatic bilateral pneumothorax, and ecchymosis" to some doctor on the other end of the invisible line.

Matters got worse as they watched these young clinicians stick people with needles and inject them with drugs, sometimes raising the dead.

Many of the old-timers tossed in the towel when women began wearing the same uniform and doing the same work (I once heard a salty old veteran say that what was then screwing up the fire service was EMS and PMS), work that a generation ago had been one of the major substances that defined them as men.

Even the enlightened change agents, who were dragging the organization into the twentieth century, had moments when they couldn't believe their ears.

One of the first paramedics was a firefighter named Albert. Albert was one of the first Native-American firefighters to come to work for the Phoenix Fire Department. Albert lived by many of the traditions and attitudes of his native people. If things got confusing at work, Albert would simply disappear for weeks at a time. When he returned from his hiatus, he was good to go, making peace, and burying the organizational stress that had sent him up the mountain.

Some of the senior managers didn't know what to do with Albert's occasional disappearances. Albert's chief (fire department issue) saw him as a good employee. He just had a different set of values and needed some time to fit into the routine (and culture) of his new career. He told his underlings to simply not pay Albert for the days he missed.

*Ears*

# The Anatomy and Physiology of Leadership

## Ears

Everyone just shook their heads when they heard that Albert had taken the paramedic's test and passed with flying colors.

Paramedic training is delivered by doctors, in a hospital setting. Albert was an atypical paramedic student. He sat in the back of the room and didn't say much. Sometimes he would show up a few minutes late. He never asked questions, and never appeared to study. Albert took the written test at the end of the first week and sent a minor shock wave through both the hospital and the EMS section of our fire department.

One of the doctors quietly suggested that Albert cheated because he scored so highly on the first test out of the gate. The first few tests in the program are designed to devastate the students. I'm sure this serves some educational purpose, but I'm not a doctor, so I can't even begin to guess.

The top 2%--the golden children, the overachievers, the best and the brightest, the clear-eyed A Shifters barely passed this test and most of the class flunked. It was a rigged game; marginal success was the best that the student could hope for. This was after studying for hours on end.

It was impossible that Albert, someone so different, could out score all of them by such a large margin. All the powerful people in the process had heard (with their own ears) their whole lives about how things worked. Their parents, teachers, mentors, and colleagues told them and reaffirmed the beliefs they all held sacred. The test also put the teachers in a position of authority. They set it up that way. People like Albert didn't do better at these kinds of things than people like them.

These weren't bad people. Like the rest of us, they simply believed the "bull" that had been repeated to them their whole lives. This group wasn't stupid either.

The fire chief's solution was to continue on, business as usual, and if Albert was somehow cheating it would eventually come to light. The doctor suggested a different plan. He would give Albert a test designed to measure intelligence and catch people who cheated. Since no one had ever seen or heard of a student doing so well on the first week's test, the decision was made to give Albert the cheater's test.

The general method behind the test was that the student got to study a list of drugs for thirty minutes. This list included the chemical make up of the drugs, along with the effect and side effects of each drug. There were dozens of drugs, creating thousands of possible answers for each question. Pharmacologists with twenty years of experience had trouble just passing this test.

# The Anatomy and Physiology of Leadership

The doctor who ran the paramedic program devised the exam for this very purpose--to catch cheaters. Albert would be exposed as a cheater and thrown out of the paramedic program. After hearing the news with their own ears, the fair-haired students could feel good about themselves again.

After the test was over no one believed their ears. Albert almost got a perfect score on the test. The doctor told the chief of the EMS division that he was convinced Albert was a genius and should be evaluated by the Mensa organization. He had administered this test to thousands of people, highly intelligent people, and none of them had scored as well. Albert had a new fan and finished the program without any further fanfare or scrutiny.

Albert was one of the smartest paramedics on the planet. I have heard the story that he is best known for over a dozen times. It isn't the one where he aced an impossible test. Less than ten people know that story, and most of our group could care less about it.

I have heard this legend (with my own ears) from a firefighter who swears he was there and witnessed the entire event. It is a tale that goes right to the heart of this body part--the ears.

The paramedics were summoned to a home where a man had just had a heart attack. The paramedics arrived on a beautiful red fire engine complete with polished brass and gold leaf scrolls.

The two emergency medical technicians (in this case the captain and engineer) and two paramedic firefighters grabbed their EMS gear and headed up to the front door. An older woman answered the door and led them into her living room, where her husband lay dying on the floor.

He was in his mid-sixties. The crew instantly recognized the classic symptoms of a heart attack--ashen gray color and profuse sweating.

The crew immediately went to work. The engineer cut the patient's shirt off while Albert wiped down the spots on the patient's chest and abdomen, where he would place the electrodes for the heart monitor. The captain put an oxygen mask on the patient and adjusted the regulator on the oxygen tank to fifteen liters per minute, its highest setting.

Albert's medic partner was searching for a vein to stick an eighteen-gauge needle in, to start an IV. During these initial few minutes, the captain interrupted the wife's endless

## The Anatomy and Physiology of Leadership

#  Ears

questions, asking her to put the cat (which was attacking their medical gear) in another room.

The distraught woman distracted by her husband's condition wouldn't listen, and the cat didn't seem interested in calling off its assault.

The engineer was doing chest compressions on the patient. Albert had secured all of his heart monitor hookups and had the engineer cease compressions so he could analyze the patient's heart rhythm. Before Albert could get a clear look at the video display on the monitor, the cat had pulled one of the leads off the patient. Albert took a swipe at the feline, causing it to disappear under the sofa, and told the woman in his calm, low voice, "Lady, your husband is dead right now. If you get the kitty cat out of our way we can probably save him."

In one ear and out the other. The woman continued her blather, neither acknowledging the crew nor securing the disruptive animal.

Albert's partner had finished hooking up the IV and was ready to start administering cardiac drugs, but he needed to know what kind of electrical activity was taking place in the patient's heart. Albert got the lead hooked up again and was running a strip off the monitor, showing the patient's fibrillating heart. The patient's only chance for survival was if the crew could shock his heart back into a normal rhythm.

The cat sprang out from under the sofa and attacked the IV tubing hooked into its master's arm. The beast dislodged the tubing and now IV fluids were flowing into the drug box. The captain kicked at the kitty, causing it to jump over the sofa.

Now the crew was screaming at the woman to capture the cat. It may have been the stress of the moment, or the woman was just an idiot, but the cat was seriously disrupting the crew's attempts at saving the man's life.

A few seconds later, the crew got everything back in order. Albert's partner was pushing cardiac drugs into the reestablished IV. The engineer was doing chest compressions and the captain was delivering large quantities of oxygen, with a football-shaped bag valve mask, hooked up to a tube that had been inserted into the patient's trachea. Albert was preparing to shock the patient's heart back into a normal rhythm with 200 joules of electricity delivered through a set of defibrillation paddles.

The crew stopped what they were doing, breaking contact with the patient, in

# The Anatomy and Physiology of Leadership

preparation for Albert delivering the lifesaving blast of electricity, when kitty showed up for another pass. The cat landed on top of the patient and hissed at Albert.

No one expected the cat to listen to them. Cats don't speak English, and even if they did, I suspect they really don't care what you have to say. The patient couldn't listen because he was dead. If the woman had only listened, what happened next could have been avoided.

Albert repositioned his energized paddles and let the cat have it. The first time I heard the story I didn't believe my ears either. It gets better.

The crew was broken from their stunned silence, when they heard the cat making very uncat like noises. Next they smelled smoldering hair. Albert casually hit the recharge button on the defib machine, waited a few seconds for the device to power up, and delivered the charge to the patient.

He studied the rhythm for a few seconds and said, "We got a normal heart beat, keep bagging him Skip."

The woman reappeared and asked, "What in the world is that horrible smell?"

What happened next was a festival of the senses. The cat shot across the living room and climbed the drapes. The cat was seriously annoyed and full of bad intentions because the shot of electricity had set it on fire. The woman shrieked as her draperies began to burn. Engineers tend to be very mechanical people, who come up with simple answers to complex problems. He grabbed an IV bag out of the drug box and quickly extinguished the drapes. Only after his captain ordered him, did he douse the cat.

The patient made a full recovery. The wife filed a complaint. After hearing the whole story, the crew's supervisor decided to do nothing. The cat survived its ordeal. Albert became a legend.

*Ears*

# The Anatomy and Physiology of Leadership

*Ears*

# *The Anatomy and Physiology of Leadership*

# Nose

# *The Anatomy and Physiology of Leadership*

*Nose*

# The Anatomy and Physiology of Leadership

# Nose

## Basic Leadership Capability

The nose is stuck out front, typically arrives early (many times first) in the leadership event and can provide an effective, and along with the gut, the quickest (actually primitive) level of early warning and ongoing information of all the body parts. The nose is best at quickly sizing up political situations, and the gut is best at evaluating physical conditions. Experienced leaders develop a refined and practiced sense of "smell."

The nose has the capability to quickly detect information/data on a more refined and subtle level than most of the other A & P body parts. Most situations, conditions and people come packaged in ways that create many different (and definitive) smells (both literally and figuratively). Literally means some people, places, and things have a physical odor. Figuratively means that others have a social, psychological, or political profile that can "smell" good or stink. Smart, old street guys/gals learn how to identify both kinds, and how to react to what the nose is sensing.

Like our other capabilities, the nose has a memory that can provide a useful frame of reference. The nose has an enormous capability to both store and recall a wide variety of both literal and figurative smells. This becomes a huge advantage in connecting past experiences of nose reactions to current conditions.

Smart "smellers" use their noses creatively to do an initial evaluation (sweep) of a situation. This odor identification must then be quickly connected to other body parts to create a continuously integrated evaluation and reaction. There are comfortable old smells; alarming smells of previous pain; interesting, intriguing new smells; and confusing situational "odors" that serve as warnings.

# The Anatomy and Physiology of Leadership

## Nose (cont.)

Many times, the smelling sense is the most acute and accurate in the very beginning of a situation or issue and can provide a fast go/no go direction/warning. Leaders must guard against smelling something, someplace, or somebody for so long that it dulls (actually anesthetizes) their smelling sense.

Leaders with a lot of seniority out in the real world probably have enlisted (and listened to) a steady stream of smart "new noses." These smelling helpers can provide important translation services that expand how we are able to evaluate a wide variety of situations.

The nose is quick in sounding an initial alarm, but many times it takes a moment for it to be very analytical. It is really good at sending a quick "something's not right" message, but generally doesn't in the very beginning indicate a lot of the details of what's out of balance. It quickly detects when a something/someone situation is packaged up and is just "not right." When it sets off and sends the alarm message to the brain, the other body parts (eyes, ears, brain) must then go to work to figure out the details of the situation.

The nose asks a different set of questions and creates a different (and faster) response than the other body parts. The nose has a high voltage (short circuit). Our nose (like our gut) is not highly evolved, but it is highly perfected--simply, it's very sensitive but not real sophisticated. It either likes or doesn't like what it smells, and it quickly detects "bad stuff"... bad money, bad relationships, bad deals, bad temptations, bad offers, etc.

Smart old soldiers got to be old and got to stay soldiers by both trusting and reacting to nose signals. Simply, when their noses start twitching, they slow down, look past the initial views, engage their brains, and instruct their feet to be careful where they are taking their other body parts, until whatever caused the alarm is checked out.

# The Anatomy and Physiology of Leadership

## Nose (cont.)

### Rules of Engagement

- Understand that people, places, and things produce "smells" that are (both literal and figurative) signals.

- Trust/react to olfactory messages (alerts/signals)--if it smells like warm cookies, go get a glass of milk... if it smells like poop, it probably is--be careful where you "step."

- Many times when you "smell a rat," it is because there is one of the little demons lurking around.

- Develop, expand, and utilize an "odor library"... continually catalog, enter, store, and refer to a wide variety of smells.

- Run a continual personal "smell test" and organizational "headline test"--recognize and respond to "funny smells."

- Continually refine/recalibrate your sense of smell based on experience, reflections, and changes in the environment.

- DSR--doesn't smell right.

- Nose works best up close.

- Pay attention to changes in smells.

- React quickly to danger/survival smells.

# The Anatomy and Physiology of Leadership

## Nose (cont.)

- Recruit other's noses to widen "smelling":

  - Run the situation by a "helper nose."
  - Watch how their "nose" reacts.
  - Ask the helper what they smell.
  - Listen and react.

- Protect/manage your nose:

  - out-of-joint (shape) prevention
  - other people's business (stay out of)
  - keep clean
  - don't look down
  - avoid sharp, direct blows
  - keep to the grindstone
  - don't thumb nose (at others)
  - keep out of air (snooty).

- Be aware if you're upwind or downwind... that position will determine if the "smell" is coming or going--react based on that position.

- Develop and refine a "nose gauge" that shows the presence, intensity, and dynamics (changes) of smells.

- Connect a standard response to a standard smell to create a standard (hopefully effective) outcome.

# The Anatomy and Physiology of Leadership

# Nose

Our nose is the organ we use to determine the correct course and proper actions we must take when faced with some new challenge. We also use our nose to first detect and then determine if something is right or not, much in the same way we use our olfactory sense to tell if A-Shift leftovers are still edible. When in doubt, have the new guy try them first.

As we work our way through life, we catalogue each new smell and experience, collecting them in our brain so we can pull that file when we run across that scent again. This is a major way we build our experience data bank.

There is an interesting contrast between your nose and your gut. We use the nose to sniff out the situation and figure out an appropriate course of action (or plan) in dealing with those conditions. The nose only works when you are alert and awake. The gut works on its own special, subconscious level, collecting subliminal information from all of the other body parts and sending a hunch to the brain.

It may sound like semantics, but there is a difference between something not smelling right, and something not feeling right.

Some cooks only know the beans are burning after they smell them. Chefs sense (a hunch from the gut) when they are low and add fluids before they burn.

The nose is oftentimes used to describe a person's talent or ability. Reporters who have a knack for breaking big stories are said to have a nose for the news. These folks have spent a long time covering the news and have become very good at what they do, because they have worked hard at honing the skills required to be a top-notch journalist. This is no different from any other occupation. The more we understand our work and the longer we do it, the better we become doing it.

Fire fighting has been the bread and butter service delivery ritual of the fire service for the last several thousand years. Fire fighting is hazardous work. We have worked long and hard to refine these operations, making them safer for our members. Many firefighters are alive and well today because they followed (and listened) to their noses when something "smelled funny." During the last forty or so years, many of our organizations have expanded our service delivery menus. We have added emergency medical response and transportation, hazardous materials response, and technical rescue to our repertoires.

Most of these new service types just kind of fell to us because no one can deliver quickly-assembled teams of qualified workers (firefighters) to the scene of an emergency as well as the fire service. First when seconds count.

# The Anatomy and Physiology of Leadership

# Nose

One of the challenges we faced when we took on these new service-delivery types was they were significantly different from our standard, structural fire attack. Using the same tactics for hazardous materials incidents that we use for structural fire fighting will eventually get us killed. After a short period of time, we figured out that half of the people killed by incidents involving hazardous materials and technical rescue scenarios were the rescuers.

This caused our fire-service leaders to develop a new approach and philosophy for handling these types of incidents. Our noses did not have enough exposure or knowledge to safely deal with the new hazards we faced when responding to these types of incidents. Today hazmat and technical rescue teams represent the cutting edge for incident evaluation, operation, and safety. The training, tools, equipment systems, and most importantly the firefighters who specialize in these activities are among our best and brightest.

A busy freeway is a really bad place to have a tanker truck full of hazardous material roll over and catch on fire. The vehicle blocks traffic and the hazardous liquid cargo gushes out of its damaged container, catching on fire and burning in pretty hues of violet and blue, accented by smoke with a green and red tint. If the tanker happens to be uphill of the blocked traffic, the burning liquid has the very real potential of burning the blocked motorists alive. Even if fire doesn't break out, and everyone survives unscathed, they will all be late in getting where they were going.

Myron had been a member of the fire department for a long time, the last fifteen years spent as a battalion chief. Myron, along with an engine and ladder company, was en route to a reported car accident on the freeway.

His nose (and eyes) told him that the plume of pastel-colored fire burning into emerald and red-tinted smoke meant bad news. This wasn't going to be an ordinary vehicle fire. Pastel fire and plaid smoke was a pretty good indication that some type of hazardous material was involved.

Myron was a mile from the scene when he upgraded the assignment to a first-alarm hazardous (more engines, ladders, and special haz-mat response units).

The first-arriving engine company navigated its way through the maze of backed-up traffic and made its way to the scene. The captain reported, "Engine 10 on the scene with an overturned tanker on the freeway. We have product leaking and active fire that appears to involve hazardous materials. We are attacking the fire with a foam line. Engine 10 will be Freeway Command."

# The Anatomy and Physiology of Leadership

Myron was next to arrive. It took him a couple of minutes to maneuver his sedan around the traffic bedlam and find a position with a decent view of the incident site. The accident had blocked all lanes of traffic, but Engine 10's attack line was doing a good job of knocking down the fire. Myron noticed that several people were standing on the side of the roadway, vomiting over the guardrail. He contacted the captain of Engine 10, took command then radioed alarm. "Battalion 1 to Alarm… be advised that I'm transferring command. Engine 10 is controlling the fire, and we have several victims puking in the emergency lane. Give me a second-alarm medical."

Myron had a pretty straightforward plan. The bulk of the fire was knocked down and the hazardous materials team was starting to arrive and get set up. He was going to have them handle all of the details involved with the leaking tanker.

Companies were reporting that a dozen or so motorists had fallen ill from inhaling small amounts of the green and red smoke. Myron determined that the eight engine and four ladder companies assigned to the incident could treat the dozen known patients, and handle the three or four last-minute patients who always seemed to show up at this kind of event.

Over the years, he had developed a theory that among the "special responders" were legal strike teams (four lawyers in Lincoln Town cars), who drove around listening to police and fire scanners in anticipation of creating new opportunities for themselves.

Myron was making notes on his tactical work sheet after verifying with Alarm that he had twelve ambulances responding to the scene, when everything got dark. It felt like a solar eclipse was taking place.

Myron turned his head to look out the window of his sedan and stared into the groin of a large human being. As Myron's gaze moved skyward, he saw the high-polish gleam of a black leather gun belt, which showed the care and love one usually reserved for an adored grandmother. It looked like the cop had a bazooka in his gleaming holster. The policeman was so tall he had to take several steps backward in order to bend down low enough to look into the open window of the old battalion chief's sedan to tell him that they needed to talk.

Before Myron could climb out of his car, the haz-mat sector officer cleared him over the radio and let him know they had identified the now smoldering material in the freshly extinguished tanker as tetra-methyl-death. The freeway would need to be shutdown for a while longer.

*Nose*

## The Anatomy and Physiology of Leadership

# Nose

Myron cut an imposing figure as he climbed out of his car. He had a clipboard that held his tactical work sheet--the written document that reminded him where the twelve companies on the incident had been assigned, including which hospital each of the seven ambulances were taking their vomiting patients.

Because the incident had two major components, dealing with the haz-mat problem and treating and transporting a double-digit number of patients, two tactical radio channels were put into operation.

This required Myron to talk over, and listen to, two separate portable radios. Both radios were clipped to the belt that held the gray-haired battalion chief's size thirty-eight pants firmly underneath his prodigious belly. Myron was in the full shade cast by the large cop as he navigated the ten feet that separated them.

Myron stole a quick glance at the snarl of traffic that was backed up as far as the eye could see before devoting his full attention to the cop.

The guardian of state-owned freeways was a sight to behold. He stood in excess of 6 1/2 feet tall and weighed just shy of 300 pounds. His starched uniform had to be tailored to fit his freakish proportions. His thighs were almost the same diameter of his 36-inch waist. His trousers and long-sleeved shirt were camel color. The Arizona state flag patches sewn to shoulders of his shirt looked small, as they stretched to contain a set of cantaloupe-sized shoulders. Everything on the cop looked freshly minted. The crowning touch was the Smokey the Bear hat that covered his short, military-style haircut. The cop did not smile when Myron greeted him with, "God damn son, what the hell did your mama feed you?"

"My name is Lieutenant Chase of the Arizona Department of Public Safety. According to Arizona revised statutes (state law) 1507-A, we have jurisdiction of any incident that takes place on a state-owned freeway. I am the ranking officer on scene. That puts me in charge of this incident. Our main priority is to get this traffic en route. I want you to move your fire trucks out of the way. Your people are blocking traffic."

Just because you are exposed to something, doesn't mean you have a nose for it. This wasn't the first time the cop had seen a fire department operation, but that didn't make him the number one choice to manage a multifaceted, hazard-zone operation.

All the cop really cared about was getting the traffic moving again. The last thing Myron cared about was getting the traffic moving again.

# The Anatomy and Physiology of Leadership

Myron had been an active participant in these types of events for over twenty-five years and knew that traffic wouldn't be moving past the wreckage for at least another hour. Good hazardous materials teams did not mark time with a watch, so much as they did by the changing seasons.

Myron knew that arguing with the goliath cop was pointless. His nose was also fine-tuned enough to know that the cop only thought he wanted to be in charge. Myron stepped closer and put his arm around the big man, causing him to momentarily recoil.

Myron told him, "Thank god you finally showed up." Myron reached down and pulled both radios off of his belt and pushed them and the clipboard toward the officer saying, "I've got treatment on channel 7. They've transported six patients and have five more waiting, but were having trouble finding hospitals that can take them. We got the fire out, but the hazmat team is still trying to contain the runoff from the tanker. They're on channel 11; that's the radio with the funny looking antenna. Don't be intimidated when they start using long chemical names; I don't know what the hell they're talking about either."

The next few seconds were a dance where Myron tried to make the cop take the radios and clipboard. Every time Myron advanced, the cop backed up until the officer ended the waltz with a large hand placed in the middle of the feisty battalion chief's chest.

"As the commander of this incident I order you to remain in charge until you have completed your fire department activities. My officers will continue to manage traffic control. Please notify me when you are finished. That is all."

Myron giggled as he climbed back into his sedan, his nose full of the smell of car exhaust and burned blacktop. He never saw "Captain Marvel" again.

# The Anatomy and Physiology of Leadership

*Nose*

# The Anatomy and Physiology of Leadership

# Mouth

# The Anatomy and Physiology of Leadership

*Mouth*

# The Anatomy and Physiology of Leadership

# Mouth

## Basic Leadership Capability

Our mouth gives us the basic audible capability to make various noises.  Some of those noises we call "talk."  We use talk to express ourselves vocally, to engage in conversation, and to use verbal communication to connect and interact with others.  Effective leaders use speaking as a piece of an integrated, balanced communications package that (ideally) increases mutual understanding and brings people closer together.  They realize that effective speaking must be interpersonal and that by itself, one-sided verbal communication can sometimes work against effective understanding, and that ineffective vocal stuff can actually separate and isolate people.

Leaders must realize that they own what they say.  The memory of words many times may last longer than any physical action that a boss may take.  Talking can be (and generally is) the most self-seductive and potentially damaging A & P component--leaders with unbalanced, goofy egos generally torture those around them by falling in love with their own voices.

There is a natural (and dangerous) inclination that the disconnected action of your mouth can overpower and shut down your other A & P components.  When this occurs, blab masters will naturally stop using their eyes and ears, so they miss the reaction of the listener (which is the most important part of talking).  Effective interpersonal communication requires practiced discipline that balances the effective operation of other body parts when the mouth is engaged.  Talk is a powerful leadership tool and like most powerful tools, it has the potential to produce both beautiful results and great pain and harm, based on how it is used.

# The Anatomy and Physiology of Leadership

## Mouth (cont.)

Lots of times when our eyes don't like what we see, our ears don't approve of what we hear, someone hurts our feelings (heart), or we have a strong personal opinion, we will use our mouth to vocally respond to the reaction to the input from that other body part.

We *must* develop the ability to control our mouth, because *not* doing this causes more routine, recurring problems (and pain) than any other A & P mistake. Simply, most boss screwups involve (in some way) an "I wish I hadn't said that" mistake.

When a boss is upset with someone, they can generally control their urge to physically smack(!) that person because it is socially, organizationally, and legally frowned upon. But, can that same boss control their urge to smack that person vocally? If the boss does deliver the verbal smack, that response will probably live forever in the relationship and in the organizational folklore.

Smart communications instinctively and automatically force you to *both* ask and answer the standard (brain before mouth) review questions. This approach will work against quickly saying something (i.e., blurt) that feels good when we are angry, upset, or when someone hurts our feelings (and we take it personally).

While this dysfunctional response (taking it personally = ego centered) causing us to say something with a "sharp edge" is natural, it only feels good until the other person does exactly the same thing, and verbally bashes us back. Their defensive response makes us even more angry, upset, or hurt, and now the process goes from dumb to dumber... and so on. It only takes a nano second to answer the review questions (if we practice). That nano-second interruption can be a huge personal performance advantage because it can prevent the mega pain of dumb and dumber--mouth demons thrive on the tongue; they die in the brain--real simple, real important.

# The Anatomy and Physiology of Leadership

## Mouth (cont.)

### Rules of Engagement

- Think before you speak; always try to be articulate, thoughtful, and persuasive (basic stuff like please, thank you, you're welcome is always nice).

- Don't talk just for the sake of talking: If you can't improve silence, be quiet; always balance knowing what you're talking about with talking--if you don't know what to say, simply shut up... sometimes, silence is the best answer.

- Regulate voice tone, timing, and level to match the situation.

- Don't yell at the workers:

  - It makes them mad.
  - Everyone is less effective.
  - You look stupid.
  - They remember it (a long time).

- Prevent harm: If you can't say something nice, be very careful (call your mom; she'll tell you what to say/what *not* to say).

- Don't talk about things that are no one else's business (i.e., mind your own business).

- Realize that some things are better left unsaid--it's okay (and a lot of times really smart) to have an unexpressed thought.

- Control your "blurt valve"--some of the smartest (and most powerful) words are the ones we never say.

# The Anatomy and Physiology of Leadership

## Mouth (cont.)

- Don't bite off more than you can chew.

- A smart guy said: "Most of my problems were the result of what went into and came out of my mouth."

# The Anatomy and Physiology of Leadership

## Mouth

Our bodies give us substance, person, and attach us to this physical dimension. People and other life forms identify us by our material being. Our body is all we have that connects us to civilization, but what comes out of our mouth defines us as an individual. Verbal communication (via the old pie hole) is responsible for most everything that has happened over the course of human history.

Successful people know when to speak, what to say, when to shut up and listen, and most importantly when to act on what has been communicated.

The mouth and ears must coexist in proper measure. It's a lot like the relationship in baseball between the catcher and pitcher-- without both pieces working together, you have a guy throwing a ball at an umpire or a man squatting over home plate waiting for someone to bring the heat. Bring the two together in proper proportions and you're playing America's game.

Much of the way the world views us is based on the things we say. Smart, dumb, funny, enlightened, nice, and nasty are some of the qualities that are a product of what comes out of our mouths. Once our circle of friends and acquaintances have pigeonholed our personality, anything that falls outside of that narrow definition of who we are will generally shock and confuse them. Another inescapable product of what comes out of our mouth is that it lives forever. Say something outlandish enough, and it will take on a life of its own.

Ten years ago the fire department began sending its fire investigators through the police academy, because on rare occasions a fire investigator would be required to arrest arson suspects. Fire investigators are fire captains. You are asking for trouble when you take a group of veteran firefighters and send them through the rigid system designed to shape and mold brand new police officers.

The police recruits march, shine their shoes, and call everyone sir. The fire captains show up forty-five minutes late, with a sack of chorizo and egg burros, sit in the back of the room, and call everyone sweetheart.

Police recruits were receiving written reprimands for pocketing extra change they found in the soda machine, while fire captains merrily interrupted instructors in the middle of class, asking when they were going to get to shoot the guns. After the first week, the commander of the academy met with the captains and pleaded with them to at least show up on time.

# *The Anatomy and Physiology of Leadership*

The fire department's role in the community is to keep the village from burning down, bandage wounds, and make the occasional suggestion. The cops, on the other hand, arrest people.

They (the cops) have a very strict set of rules (called laws) that they enforce. They are also sanctioned by the community to shoot people who break the main rules. Both organizations fall under the umbrella of public safety, but in many ways we are very different from one another.

Ever since the fire investigator position was expanded to include being a sworn member of law enforcement, it changed the process that a fire captain has to go through to become one. In the old days, all you needed was a bushel full of seniority as a captain to join the ranks of an investigator.

In today's world you have to go through a much more elaborate process to snoop around the inside of burned-out buildings.

A major part of this process includes undergoing a polygraph test. This is a normal piece of the cop world. Police departments around our country perform thousands of polygraph tests on their employees every day. This is one of those rituals that serves two purposes-- having to prove you follow the rules you are being paid to enforce and that you remember you work for the man. He can drag your ass downtown and hook you up to the box whenever he feels like it.

As a rule, firefighters are not required to undergo lie detector tests; it has never been part of our entrance requirements. The deputy chief in charge of the fire investigators assembled the group of investigator "wannabes" and forewarned them, "If you guys can't pass a lie detector test, save yourself the time and effort and drop out now. The cops administer the lie detector test, and they will ask you every question you can imagine, and some that you can't. I've known all of you for years and am fairly confident that some of you should avoid this test like the plague."

The chief was using his mouth to help four or five of the misguided (or at least uninformed) captains who he knew didn't stand a chance of beating the lie detector.

The early warning system was personalized after the meeting, when one of the current investigators took several of the new candidates off to the side and told them some of the questions they could expect. This in no way is meant to imply that we have a small group of hardened criminals in our midst. In fact, it really goes to the heart of how stupid the lie

# The Anatomy and Physiology of Leadership

detector test is. Does it really matter if you had a personal relationship with a chicken some twenty years ago? I think not.

There is a big difference between having a colorful past and being stupid. One of the nameless investigator candidates pressed forward after several warnings. He mistook a polygraph test (being administered by a cop none the less) as a confessional. This rocket scientist sat there with all the wires hooked up to him and voluntarily admitted to the commission of serious misdeeds. It got so bad that the cop administering the test excused himself halfway through the ordeal, in order to call his boss for direction. If the test was allowed to continue, he was worried that he may have to actually arrest the "subject" (that's what cops call the people they are investigating).

The ranking cop, on the other end of the line told his subordinate to immediately terminate the test and excuse the candidate. The boss man then called his counterpart in the fire department and explained the situation. That is another story entirely.

Compare our misguided captain's use of his mouth against the polygraph experience that one of his associates had that very same day. Same job interview, same polygraph administrator, same set of questions, but a different outcome.

Halfway through the test, the examiner told Captain #2 that his answers appeared to be evasive. The captain shook his head and told the tester that he was telling the whole truth. As the test continued the proctor restated that the machine indicated that the "subject" (that word again) was not being entirely truthful. The captain told the examiner there must be something wrong with his machine because, "My mamma didn't raise no liars and I ain't going sit by while you dis my mamma, you !@#$%&". The test was quickly concluded without any phone calls to anyone's boss.

The purpose of this little section of the story is to highlight the differences in the way people manage their mouth, when faced with the same situation. Captain #1's mouth management caused him great pain in the end. Captain #2 controlled his mouth in a way that cost him nothing. Neither one of the candidates was selected to become an investigator, but that really isn't a big deal when one considers that neither one of them will ever be the Queen of England, and that is a much greater loss.

Effective people owe much of their success to how well they manage what comes out of their mouth. Great leaders always seem to know what to say, along with when to say it. Just as importantly, they know when to lay back, watch, and listen to what is going on, while keeping their mouth shut.

# The Anatomy and Physiology of Leadership

# Mouth

During my very short time in college, I took a psychology class. We spent a very painful afternoon discussing the three personas that make up each of us--the way we see ourselves, the way others see us, and the way we really are.

I believe that the way we manage our mouth has more to do with the way the outside world views us, than all of the other body parts combined. You do not have to hook a person up to a lie detector to know whether or not they are full of "bull."

Our human resources department made the statement that it was harder to become a Phoenix firefighter than it was to get accepted to the University of Arizona Medical School. I have no reason to doubt them. Both are fine organizations, but ours doesn't require amassing huge debt and carrying exorbitant malpractice insurance. Also, we have a better pension plan and nurses are friendlier towards us.

We are very selective about who we hire, because we can be. Every year thousands of highly-qualified applicants compete for a handful of positions. Our new hires are spectacular individuals. This makes the occasional inappropriate hire very glaring.

The process to become a firefighter has become quite complex, but in the end it still comes down to a thirty-minute oral interview. If a candidate successfully navigates the political minefield of gaining entrance into the training academy, they land a thirty-two year career, which includes full benefits and a lifetime pension upon retirement.

If your mouth can dazzle for half an hour, you are set for life. This is akin to going to Las Vegas, having a chance encounter with a total stranger that begins with all-out intoxication, leading into sinning of a magnitude they talk about in the Bible, and ending in a marriage performed by an Elvis impersonator, ordained by the Universal Life Church. This is not the model most successful marriages are built on, but for some reason, it is a similar (if not longer) time line that most municipal fire departments use to choose their lifetime members.

I have been around a little while and have seen my share of firefighter candidates ("wannabes") come through the transom. Many of them hang out at fire stations because they think it will help them get hired.

The intelligent ones seek out the newest firefighters to find out what they said during

# The Anatomy and Physiology of Leadership

the thirty-minute dance that got them hired. The vast majority of these individuals are young, smart, nice people with beautiful teeth, smooth skin, and sparkly eyes. It must be difficult for the members of the interview board/selection committee, because these people all begin to look alike and sound the same. It is my experience that most of these people would (and do) make excellent firefighters.

When meeting a person for the first time, it takes no more than five minutes of conversation to establish how you will feel about them for the rest of your life. One of the rare exceptions to this rule is quiet people. We all have friends and acquaintances who don't say much. These people are generally described somewhere between mysterious and intelligent.

The first time I met firefighter candidate Dexter, I pegged him as a thoroughbred kiss ass. He would not stop talking. He pumped so much syrup-laden sunshine into the room, it felt like he was eulogizing the people he was talking about. I called my father (our Department's fire chief) to make sure he was still alive.

This personality trait was amplified by his smug and condescending style. He conveys the impression that you don't know that the saccharine pushing out of his every pore and word is the slightest bit insincere.

The first time I met him was at a fire station that housed a dozen firefighters. Everyone felt like bathing after he left.

Much to all of our shock and dismay, firefighter candidate Dexter somehow got through the entry obstacle course and became Firefighter Dexter. It came as no surprise that his recruit training class pioneered a new ritual, complete with its own trophy.

Every Friday, the class would vote for the "Kiss Ass of the Week." After Firefighter Dexter won the trophy for the fifth or sixth straight week he went to the Director of Training to have an end put to his weekly award. "Kiss Ass of the Week" doesn't fit in with our organizational philosophy of "Be Nice" so the award was terminated.

The dilemma we are faced with is Firefighter Dexter can perform capably in the role of a firefighter. It is not against the law to act like a rectum weevil, but it is next to impossible to terminate a person's employment for being a brown-nosing toad. What Dexter lacks in mouth skills, he compensates for with energy, hustle, ambition, and a sense of his own

*Mouth*

# The Anatomy and Physiology of Leadership

superiority. You almost have to admire his drive.

Whenever his name is mentioned, people cringe; yet, that doesn't slow him down. Most of the world's truly wonderful megalomaniacs had humble beginnings. I'm sure the other house painters thought the new kid, Adolph Hitler, was a bubble off, but he didn't let the opinion of others hold him back.

Being a mouth Nimrod does not limit how far one can go organizationally. Many organizations are headed by CEOs just like Dexter.

Every couple of years we give a captain's test. The difference between hiring a new firefighter and the testing process for the captain's position is that the captain candidates are well known to the members sitting on the interview boards. It's much more difficult to snowball a group of people who have known you for the last decade.

Still, this remains an imperfect process. Engineer Clayton was one such individual. The first ten years of his career he used his mouth to great effect in nurturing, establishing, and maintaining his reputation as a know-it-all. He was well known for telling anyone willing to listen that he was the smartest man on the Phoenix Fire Department. He earned his nickname "sexual intellectual" (he knew f'ing everything).

The interview board was having this same conversation as Clayton sat in the waiting room. Clayton was called in for his interview. It was pretty much a typical captain's interview, up until the closing statement. Clayton was passing, but he positioned to finish in the bottom percentile of the list, which would come as a surprise only to Clayton.

Then it happened. Clayton told the interview board that he had done a lot of soul searching over the last year. Several of his family members had died. He left things unsaid with them because they could no longer stand to share the same room with him.

More than a few members of the fire department had taken the time to sit him down and tell him they did not want to work with him because he was always running his mouth. The final straw was his wife telling him that she and the kids cherished their time away from him during his twenty-four hour work shifts.

# The Anatomy and Physiology of Leadership

He told the board he had come to realize he was a pompous, loud mouth and wouldn't blame them if he failed the test all together. All he wanted was the chance to redeem himself and start anew.

The board was so moved by Clayton's confession, they erased the basement-level score for which he had worked his entire career, and replaced it with a set of numbers that would put him in a position to be promoted, just before the list expired. Redemption for Clayton was brief; he is now known as "Captain Sexual Intellectual."

We all have Dexters and Claytons whom we live and work around. We will not agree with (nor even like) everyone that crosses our path. This is part of life, and we need to develop coping mechanisms for dealing with these individuals.

On a personal level this makes us better people. Organizationally, it makes us stronger when we tolerate (and even accept) other people who occasionally repulse our personal and social sensibilities. It also grants us the liberty and right to make our own occasional mouth mistakes.

# The Anatomy and Physiology of Leadership

*Mouth*

# The Anatomy and Physiology of Leadership

## Face

# The Anatomy and Physiology of Leadership

## Face (cont.)

manage their own facial messages, they also develop the ability and awareness to understand the dynamics of facial expressions and the facial dynamics in others.

There isn't much we can do about how our face looks (what we got is what we got); however, there is a lot we can do about how we control the expression that is on that face--most people will react a lot more to the expression than the face itself (thank heavens). Skillful communicators use other's reactions to their expression as an interpersonal "mirror." This facial feedback requires an increased level of self awareness, personal evaluation, and response. As we receive this feedback, we must make whatever adjustments that are required to create and send an appropriate and effective facial message to fit that particular (other) person and situation. This capability becomes a big part of our "social radar"--this "radar" is how we observe, process, and then effectively react to how what (and how) we are saying and doing is affecting others.

We must also use that personal radar to develop an understanding of how our natural "face picture" looks and how others typically react to that very individual look. We must then adjust our expression to fit each situation.

Every face just naturally looks its own special way... serious, youthful, pretty, plain, old, sad, funny, scary, etc. Sometimes that natural look fits the situation (and is an advantage), and other times we must consciously change our natural expression and use our other body parts to effectively fit the current situation.

Sometimes, a person's face looks very stern, but completely changes (becomes more friendly) when they smile. So smiling becomes very important for that person to send a positive and more inviting message.

# The Anatomy and Physiology of Leadership

## Face (cont.)

Another person could have a naturally cheerful looking face and would have to develop using a more serious expression to effectively connect in a situation that was more intense. Simply, we can't change the basic architecture of our face, but we can control our expression and use our other A & P parts to send an effective message that fits what our face is facing.

### Rules of Engagement

- Be aware that your face is pretty much always visible and continually sends a message--choose that message carefully and consciously.

- Choose an appropriate expression that is in tune with the situation and is sending with the message you want to send. Know when it is effective to show your emotions and when it is better not to show them.

- Realize the huge impact of nonverbal communication-- your face is a picture (worth 1,000 words).

- Stay consciously connected to your expression and how others are reacting... be sure your eyes are open (and engaged) when your mouth is open.

- Watch others as they interact. Study how their facial expressions affect the situation they are in... these are free lessons we can apply to ourselves.

- Use your facial expression to encourage, support, connect, and facilitate effective listening by sending a positive message for others to open up and communicate.

# The Anatomy and Physiology of Leadership

## Face (cont.)

- Use your face to reinforce/complement your words/speech.

- Don't be two faced--be genuine.

- If you're happy, let your face in on it... smile.

- Know when to show your face.

- Put your best face (expression) forward to fit the situation.

- Understand that playing poker and walking into a surprise party in your honor each require a different facial expression management approach.

- Smile a lot (it's healthy).

# The Anatomy and Physiology of Leadership

## Face

We are best known for our face. It's how we tell one another apart, and the reason that Washington's mug (as opposed to his knees) is on the one-dollar bill. The eyes may be the window to the soul, but the face is the billboard that contains them. The most profound and important communications are not spoken, they are displayed by the look on our face. The verbal description for feelings of love, terror, hysteria, and boredom can never capture the true meaning of those emotions, as well as the look on the face of the person experiencing those sensations. It's pretty tough to describe the taste of rocky-road ice cream.

Fire departments across the world provide an invaluable service to the people. There is a certain comfort in knowing that if you, a loved one, a friend, or a total stranger is having a problem, help is a few minutes away. The fire service motto of "first, when seconds count" is an anomaly in an era of automated phone menus, having to schedule service appointments between eight and noon (generally a month in advance), and completing a stack of forms for the most routine service visit. You cannot assign a value to having the faces of four highly-qualified firefighters show up at your front door when your world is collapsing around you.

The six of us had faces that could have been cast for the western, *The Good, the Bad, and the Ugly*. The captain and engineer owned the oldest faces, ones that had been seasoned by lives spent in the desert sun. Their expressions change very little during the course of a shift, ranging from amused smiles to a kind of reflective boredom.

The other firefighter assigned to the engine was just beginning his career. His facial expression bounced around, going from confusion to concentration, occasionally punctuated with the surprised look of a new discovery.

On this day, my face was best described as average. I was born with a gigantic head and face. My childhood pictures look like some mad scientist stuck Marlon Brando's head on a two-year old's torso. I had the cranial/body proportions of a bobble-head doll. Many of my family members felt I was destined for a career as a television newscaster or the circus. Thankfully, my body caught up with my head and face.

A person would have to have less than perfect vision to describe the group of us as ruggedly handsome. The paramedics assigned to the rescue were another matter. Both of them had slender wrists and ankles, causing their

# The Anatomy and Physiology of Leadership

# Face

sculpted physics to look bigger than their actual size. Their perfectly shaped heads were adorned with movie star faces. The two of them were prettier than a roomful of cheerleaders.

I don't remember what the six of us were doing that afternoon when we were dispatched on an "unknown medical." This is the way our Alarm Room dispatches medical calls, when they don't know what's happening, but feel the call warrants sending a unit to check it out. Because the caller was hysterical, the incident was dispatched with a paramedic component.

We drove down the street of a middle class neighborhood lined with big shade trees, arriving at a small bungalow style house, and found a woman in her mid-thirties sobbing uncontrollably on the steps of her front porch. She had a pretty face. We did what any group of men would do for a crying woman, patted her on the shoulder and told her it would be all right. She knew we were full of it, but she was either too upset or too kind to say anything about it.

After several minutes of being a caring nurturer, I began to wonder why this hysterical woman had a plate of cookies. I then started to wonder if she would mind if I had one of them. She was finally able to tell us that she was not an unknown medical; it was the woman inside that we needed to check.

The crying lady was the next-door neighbor. She didn't have anything wrong with her, medically speaking that is. She was very upset over what she had just witnessed.

About once a week the crying lady (I don't know what else to call her) went over to visit her kindly and elderly next-door neighbor. She would bring over a tray of cookies, while granny made a pot of tea, and they would just sit and visit for a while.

On this particular day, she did not get a response when she knocked at the front door. The neighbor ladies each had a key for one another's front doors. Feeling uncertain over the status of her maternal friend, the cookie lady let herself in.

I can see her now, unlocking the door, nervously breeching the sanctity of the old woman's home, calling out her friend's name, wearing concern and trepidation on her face, as she wondered if her tea-time buddy was all right. She got no response as she wandered deeper into her neighbor's home. Her safari came to an end in the bedroom, where she found granny.

The old gal spent her final moments sitting on the edge of her bed. In the act of getting undressed she suffered some type of medical episode that ended her life. The old lady was wearing a brassiere, a very smart plaid wool

# The Anatomy and Physiology of Leadership

skirt with white hose, and black orthopedic granny shoes when she died. She collapsed straight back into the center of the bed with her feet on the floor. I assumed that she died immediately.

This isn't what had the crying lady out of sorts. The old woman did not have one of those, "I went peacefully in my sleep" looks, on her face. Her gray hair was frizzy, like she had taken her bun out and fluffed her hair vigorously right before she keeled over. Two giant blue eyes started at us. She did not have any skin left on her face. All of the flesh covering the old woman's face had been picked clean, leaving the smooth white bone and little else.

The fact that the rest of her body was completely intact made no sense. She had a head like the crypt keeper. Other than the skull, crazy hair, and the two gigantic blue eye orbs, staring at nothing in particular, the old lady looked like she was just taking a short rest.

As the six of us stood there with stunned looks on our faces, trying to figure out what had happened, we heard a small bark emanating from under the bed.

Bad dog. I have never trusted small dogs. After Granny died she was unable to feed Fluffy. Fluffy tried to wake her owner by licking her face. Over time, licking progressed into nibbling, which led to eating.

Once a small lap dog tastes human flesh, they cannot be trusted around people ever again (I remember this from an early horror movie).

This call had all of the elements of a really good urban legend. If I hadn't seen it with my own eyes, I would have been very doubtful the subsequent dozen or so times that I've heard it recanted around fire stations, over the past twenty years.

After the group of us had gotten over the initial shock of seeing the faceless corpse, we turned our attention to the crying cookie lady on the front porch. She had never seen anything like this and needed some kind of answer.

The old gal had passed away and no longer had any use for the sack of skin and bones that she once resided in. It's not like the obnoxious little dog ate her alive.

We did all we could do for the crying neighbor lady, which amounted to telling her that her friend had died while sitting on her bed. It is the first (and only) time I have been involved in telling someone's friend that the victim felt no pain and had been consumed by her pet, long after she met her maker.

*Face*

# Face

This helped a little bit, but I'm sure she still has those nasty images pop into her mind every now and then.

She also remembered how nice all those firemen, with the kind faces, were to her. We became a temporary outlet for her cookies after granny checked out.

# The Anatomy and Physiology of Leadership

# Hand

# The Anatomy and Physiology of Leadership

*Hand*

# The Anatomy and Physiology of Leadership

# Hand

## Basic Leadership Capability

A unique human capability is that we humanoids can touch our index finger to our thumb.  Based on being able to do this, we can play the guitar, tie our shoes, and pinch parts of our workers that a bunch of grumpy characters in black dresses say are (legally and politically) unpinchable.

The hand is the actual (and symbolic) component that has the capability to create some tactile, physical outcome.  That outcome requires the leader to physically use their hand to create an action/effect.  Such physical action can be directed toward a mechanical activity like writing, using electronic stuff, managing business materials, manipulating tools/equipment, etc. That physical activity can also be directed toward some human contact that connects the leader to others, and typically involves positive things like shaking hands, hugging, embracing, patting, caressing, waving, pointing, holding hands, and making arm/hand gestures.

Physical contact can also involve negative actions that hurt others like hitting, slapping, choking, and generally physically and sexually harassing and assaulting others.  While leaders have only the limited physical capability of a single person and depend mostly on others to do the manual labor of the enterprise, they are always highly influential people who (typically) can (and do) have a profound effect on others.  Therefore, how they take action and "touch" people and things attracts a lot of attention.  Their actions are very observable and can have a major and very enduring positive or negative effect.

Leaders who want to stick around a long time had better learn what, where, when, and who to touch and what, where, when, and who *not* to touch.  They must realize that virtually everything they

# The Anatomy and Physiology of Leadership

## Hand (cont.)

- Know when to hang on and when to let go (if you break it, you buy it).

- Do/be/act nice (helping hand)... actions speak louder than words.

- As a leader, don't touch just because you can--keep your hands to yourself.

- Practice "smooth moves" when you touch something/somebody:
  - well timed
  - not jerky/scary
  - positive/nice
  - creates positive feeling/memory
  - no harm.

- Don't let the hand do stuff that hurts the body--yours or someone elses. Don't let the hand put junk in the body: booze, drugs, bad food, too much food, etc.

- Having to hit people over the head (with your hand) to get things done is a sign that you should use some other body parts differently/more effectively.

# *The Anatomy and Physiology of Leadership*

# Hand

Surviving the day is a universal goal for most people. The end of each workday should bring the next. Most training programs are geared around completion of the task, or set of tasks, in a safe and efficient manner.

Airplane pilots are taught to always trust their instruments. This is particularly true when flying in conditions of little, or no visibility. The weather can play tricks on your eyes, but not your gauges.

One of the core training items for firefighters is to be able to follow and "read" a hoseline in total darkness. On the surface this seems like a pretty simple deal.

The following story shows that it is the little, "simple" deal that will end up saving your ass.

The strong wind had blown a fire that started in a box crusher behind the old 25,000 square-foot grocery store into the building's storage area. The fire was currently booming its way through the large attic space over the store. The building was chopped up and had a confusing layout.

Early in the fire fight, it looked like crews had confined the fire and were finishing it off. This didn't last long. The Incident Commander (IC) had gotten nothing but bad news for the last fifteen minutes, nothing was adding up, and nasty brown smoke was rolling out of the back of the building.

It was time to punt, get all the crews out of the building and accounted for, set up big, heavy, outside master streams, and watch the old grocery store burn down. Simply, it was time to "surround and drown."

"Give me emergency traffic… we're going defensive. I want all crews to exit the building and give me a PAR".

Before the IC could switch from the inside plan to the outside plan, he received a Mayday transmission from a firefighter in trouble on the inside of the building.

"Engine 14 to command, don't leave me in here alone, I'm lost in the back of the store."

The next twenty minutes were nothing but wretched. The IC only had two entrances/exits for crews to access the large grocery store, the main entrance in front of the store, on the east side of the building, and a pair of doors used to deliver stock on the south side of the store (this is where the fire originally extended into the building).

The lost firefighter (actually, two were lost in the store at the time of the first Mayday) had initially entered the store through the main

*Hand*

# The Anatomy and Physiology of Leadership

entrance, when he and his crew had pulled their attack line into the store to fight the fire.

The line had been advanced into place under relatively clear conditions (very little smoke) and snaked its way through pallets of food products.

The crew had been in the store for approximately fifteen minutes and was running low on air. They were following their attack line back outside. They were now exiting the building in heavy smoke and heat. Visibility was zero and the crew kept falling over the now smoldering pallets, losing contact with their hose line. Once separated from the line they were lost inside the large store. Making matters more dire, they were almost out of air.

Two members of Engine 14's four-person crew had made it safely outside. The engineer was the first one out. There was so much smoke pushing out of the front of the grocery store that she didn't know she had made it outside, until she had followed the hoseline all the way to where it attached into her fire truck.

After her captain made it out, he assumed the other three members of his crew were filling their air bottles at the utility truck, until he heard his firefighter call a Mayday over the radio.

After getting the radio report that a firefighter had a Mayday situation, the IC struck another alarm, gave directions to the lost firefighter, and assigned multiple Rapid Intervention Crews (RICs) to make access into both the east and south sides of the building to locate the lost firefighters.

The rescue operation was backed up with a coordinated fire attack to keep the fire at bay (as much as possible) and buy rescue crews time to locate and remove the trapped men.

The doors on the south side of the store were used for deliveries and led into a storage and vegetable prep area in the back of the store. A second floor had been added for more storage area, packing the rear of the store with merchandise.

The four-person RIC advanced it's attack line into the building. This line served the dual purpose of protecting them from the fire and keeping them connected to their exit out of the building. If they became separated from the line, they would become as lost as the firefighters they were searching for.

During the after-incident investigation, one of the firefighters on the RIC assigned to the south rescue sector described the conditions.

# The Anatomy and Physiology of Leadership

He reported, "We had only advanced our line 10 or 15 feet inside the building. The floor was covered with smoldering debris, vegetables, and orange juice. It was like trying to walk through a burning dumpster.

You couldn't stand up and walk because the few clear spots on the floor were too slick. Crawling over the pallets and advancing the line took forever. We could see the fire burning over our heads. The ceiling was 15-, maybe 20-feet high. Letting the fire free burn gave us decent visibility, and we could see where we were going. After a few minutes, the fire would get too big and we would have to hit it with our line. This would knock down the heat, but it would create more smoke and cut our visibility down to nothing. We could hear the big steel girders that held up the roof twist and groan from the fire. Every few minutes pressurized gas cylinders, stored somewhere in the stock room, heated up and vented. When these went off, the noise was deafening. You could also hear the firefighters from nearby rescue crews screaming. I knew I was going to die."

While crews on the south side fought their own demons, the RIC team assigned to the east side of the building was running low on air and needed to exit the building. They were operating in heavy black smoke. Even with the aid of their flashlights, they could not see the hoseline they had followed into the building. This was the same line off which Engine 14 had lost two of their firefighters after they advanced into the building.

The line had been initially advanced into the building dry (not charged with water). The 200-foot long, 1 3/4-inch handline was stretched 120 feet to the seat of the fire. When the line was charged with water, the pressure caused the 80 feet of slack to coil into a series of loops down the aisle way, where the line had been extended.

When the line was initially taken into the grocery store, this wasn't a big deal because Engine 14's crew could read the labels on the soup cans, as they pulled their line past the aisles.

Fifteen minutes later, the entire grocery store had filled with thick black smoke, and anyone needing to follow this line outside to safety would be forced to travel in circles, instead of a straight line. It was like trying to follow a giant corkscrew out of the burning building.

The east rescue-crew firefighter leading his crew out of the building was disoriented after making the third circle in the coiled line. Thinking they could have somehow gotten

# The Anatomy and Physiology of Leadership

## Hand

turned around navigating through the maze of burning grocery store goods, they had an overwhelming sense of dread that they were heading deeper into the building. He had been hearing reports over his portable radio that other firefighters who were searching for the lost firefighters were now in trouble.

Uncertain, his mind filled with images of heading back into the void, running out of air, and dying in the old south Phoenix grocery store. He tried to mentally retrace their route and convince himself that he and his crew hadn't make a wrong turn; but he still fought feelings of doubt.

He had to force himself to continue down the line until they hit a coupling. It was getting hotter; the building was cracking and groaning; and the thick pressurized smoke that had swallowed everything whole was waiting for their SCBAs to run out of air, so it could kill them all. Everyone was scared.

Fourteen-short days ago, this same crew had done some informal training on the apparatus floor at their firehouse. They pulled the rigs out and pulled 300-feet of 1 1/2-inch attack line into the empty bay.

The crew dressed in full protective gear and practiced following a line in total darkness. They blackened out their SCBA face pieces and followed the line, practicing reading the couplings that attach one piece of hose to the next.

The union of the male to female coupling has distinct characteristics that indicate the direction of the apparatus--the female couplings of interior attack lines are always connected to the rig. Touch the female (follow the female to your mother) before hitting the male, and you are heading home.

The firefighter had convinced himself that they were heading in the wrong direction. He had to resist the overwhelming urge of panic when his low air alarm went off. His reptile brain told him to quit crawling in circles, get up on his hind legs, and run like hell.

At this very moment, the lost firefighter whom he and his crew were risking their lives to find was doing that exact thing, and he would soon be found dead in the back of the store.

The lead man finally reached his signpost coupling. As soon as his hand touched the hardened aluminum, he had a sinking feeling that he had led his crew too far in the wrong direction to get out alive. He slowed his breathing, ignored the assault going on all around him, and focused the touch of his hand on the 2-piece, 3-inch coupling.

# The Anatomy and Physiology of Leadership

Everything else fell away in the ten seconds it took for him to determine that he and his three comrades were heading in the right direction. A few minutes later, his SCBA ran out of air as he and the rest of his crew were taking their masks off, thirty feet outside of the building.

The four firefighters turned back to look at the death trap from which they had just escaped, as the black, pressurized smoke raging through the doorway exploded into orange flame. A simple training session, two weeks ago had given his hand the refresher course that just saved their lives.

# The Anatomy and Physiology of Leadership

*Hand*

# The Anatomy and Physiology of Leadership

## Foot

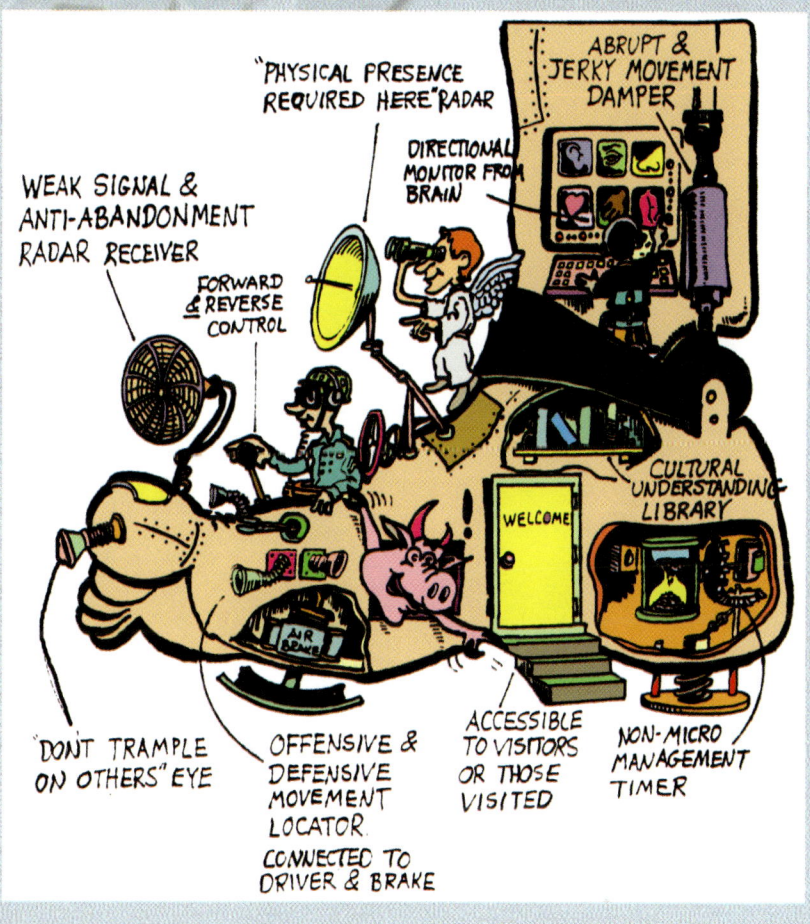

# The Anatomy and Physiology of Leadership

*Foot*

## The Anatomy and Physiology of Leadership

# Foot

### Basic Leadership Capability

A smart guy once said, "The first rule of life is showing up." Feet provide the basic capability (actual and symbolic) to move about and to actively engage in the leadership process, so the boss can effectively "show up." This mobility connects the leader with the people, places, and things that create and cause the business of the organization to occur. Where, when, and how the boss "shows up" (and "hangs out") will to a major extent influence the overall effectiveness of that person. The physical movement and the current location of the leader create an important tactical aspect (position/function) of leadership. The objective (of the tactics) is to be in the right spot at the correct time, doing the most-effective thing.

It also involves the tactics of not being in the wrong place, doing the wrong thing at the wrong time, with the wrong people (wrong = mostly ineffective... sometimes just wrong). Experienced leaders learn about these movement/location tactics and develop a sense of where to be and where not be. Such leaders use their physical presence ("sightings"), along with other A & P capabilities, to send a non-micromanagerial, supportive, and trusting message in positive situations, or a concerned and somewhat controlling message in situations that have more possible organizational risk and negative exposure.

This correct physical location capability becomes a major component in the art of leadership. The basis of this tactical leadership art is the development and operation of a personal "radar system" that continually scopes in on the situational status of that leader's

# The Anatomy and Physiology of Leadership

## Foot (cont.)

world (again, people/places/things), and provides information on the current and forecasted risks and benefits involved in being in the right place and then knowing what to do next (and next, and next...). Leadership effectiveness becomes directly connected to the leader's capability to continually and effectively connect with the currency, accuracy, and inclusiveness of this location-based "radar" process.

Effective bosses produce a basic offensive (inside) or defensive (outside) response, based on inputs from all of their body parts. They must then translate that offensive/defensive intelligence into a basic strategic position, so this becomes very important direction for the feet.

In offensive situations, the boss must get close to the operational zone and take fast, affirmative action. In defensive situations, the boss must stay back a bit and direct the action from a more remote position. This basic positioning approach becomes a big deal in both boss effectiveness and boss survival. Developing this ability will provide protection from physical, personal, and political hazards.

Sometimes bosses get involved in difficult (sad) situations where there really isn't much anyone can say that is very effective. In these situations, "being there" communicates more effectively than words. Simply, the situation outperforms any words. In these cases, making a positive difference involves just our physical presence--not what we say.

We all naturally would like to be articulate enough to always be able to express something very special that will have the magical effect of making everyone feel better.

# The Anatomy and Physiology of Leadership

## Foot (cont.)

Highly trained mental health professionals ("bar tenders") many times do not say a lot in these situations. They know that their physical presence is the most effective way to connect. Based on their training and experience, they mostly know what *not* to say. They understand that their role is to interpersonally use their presence to help that person connect with their own recovery.

These professionals do not run away from the silence of unanswerable questions ("Why did my baby die?"). They realize there are no answers to such questions. They also know that these situations typically create such a level of emotional trauma that the person will not recall what was said, as much as that the person who was with them at that time "touched" them... simply, presence heals.

Smart players know that sometimes foot action (just being there) can outperform mouth action.

## Rules of Engagement

- A big deal in leadership, as in real estate, is "location, location, location."

- Consider the message your physical location sends. Practice selected presence... be in the right place, at the right time, doing the right thing. Know both where to be and where *not* to be.

- Realize a lot happens to you (or doesn't) based on where you are (or where you are not). Know the direction to move toward or away from (offensive/defensive) and don't let the foot hurt the body.

# The Anatomy and Physiology of Leadership

## Foot (cont.)

- Use location and presence to tactically create a functional amount/level of leadership:

  - too much = overcontrol, constricted action (micromanagement)
  - too little = out of control, non-managed outcomes (abandonment).

- Know when to move your feet and when to plant them-- use your feet (location) to align others.

- MBWA (Management by Wandering Around) is handy... move proactively--"see with your feet."

- Stay agile--learn new dance steps; don't forget the old; step quickly; don't dance on your partner's toes--develop smooth steps... avoid abrupt, jerky moves.

- Be a student of the effect your presence has on the effectiveness of those around you.

- Maintain an awareness of what time it is... connect your "brain clock" with your feet to be on time.

- Always assume a leadership position:

  - Step forward/help.
  - Step in between conflict to assist, support, and resolve.
  - Be accessible.
  - Assume an observation/information point.
  - Don't step in it or on it (if you do--decon).
  - Don't jump to conclusions.
  - Don't walk on others.
  - Pace yourself.

# The Anatomy and Physiology of Leadership

## Foot (cont.)

- Be careful of being in the wrong place at the wrong time: If your feet walk you into it, they can walk you out it.

- Avoid bad situations and out-of-balance people. Know when to walk away--avoid: ugly, crazy, mean, violent, drunk, mad, nuts, no-win situations.

- Learn to use all your other body parts to cause your feet to always move toward the right place/right time and away from the wrong place/wrong time.

- Standard progression of foot development:

  - Crawl.
  - Toddle.
  - Baby step.
  - Walk.
  - Run.

- Rollover prevention (applies to lots of boss situations):

  - Slow into the curve.
  - Fast out of the curve.

- Locate yourself effectively around another's space:

  - Don't invade.
  - Understand culture.
  - Communicate with mouth/face/body.
  - Hug smartly.

# The Anatomy and Physiology of Leadership

## Foot (cont.)

- Use your feet to communicate (see/hear/speak): Remember, you must be seen to be heard.

- Adjust your foot speed to match the situation:

  - Don't walk too slowly (looks lazy).
  - Don't go too fast (looks out of control).
  - Respond to urgent incidents with a "controlled" hustle.

- Walk your talk.

# The Anatomy and Physiology of Leadership

Ninety percent of management is based on being in the right place at the right time. What you see and hear depends a good deal on where you are standing. Our feet are responsible for getting us where we need to be. Once there, the other ten percent hinges on taking the correct action, after physically positioning yourself in the right place. This ten percent makes up the core of effective leadership. The balance of this ninety/ten equation is as much art, as science.

Many of us mistakenly cling to the romantic notion that the boss must be shoulder to shoulder with the troops in the trenches. It is generally regarded as a bad sign when the field commander stops commanding because he is currently involved in hand-to-hand combat. This is a sure indicator that his troops will suffer heavy casualties. We win when the generals manage the battle, and the troops carry out the fight. That's why we have generals and privates. This model holds true for all organizational undertakings.

In the late seventies, the Phoenix Fire Department changed the way we managed the emergency incidents to which we responded. These high-octane events were (and continue to be) exciting and hazardous places to do business. Incident management was in its infancy, but it was quickly realized that this new system offered us a better and safer way to deliver (and actually manage) high-hazard customer service. The senior bosses (i.e., chiefs) of the fire department got together over a period of time to develop and implement the new incident management system. This group was made up entirely of men (no women in the suppression division in those days). They were a hands-on, smoke-in-your-hair, and soot-on-your-face group of guys.

As a young firefighter, I remember advancing a hoseline into a burning building that was fully charged with smoke. I was fully ensconced in protective gear and had trouble seeing much more than the attack line in front of me, when I felt someone pat me on the head (which was covered with a fire helmet).

I looked over to see a pair of well-shined, black uniform shoes. As my eye continued up, I could barely make out the rest of my chief, wearing his Class A uniform (blue slacks, white dress shirt, gold badge, and a pair of crossed gold bugles pinned to either side of his shirt collar). His only piece of protective gear seemed to be the cigarette he was smoking. He had slowed down to pat me on the head and tell me to "fight on," as he continued into the belly of the beast.

Our old model was to have your feet transport your eyes (and the rest of your body) to where the work was actually taking place, so you

# The Anatomy and Physiology of Leadership

could see the problem up close and personally and directly supervise the work that was taking place.

This approach worked best when the fire attack only required one or two companies. Any event requiring much beyond that level of resource quickly overwhelmed the walking boss and spiraled out of control. The new way required the boss to stay in their vehicle and manage the event over the radio.

The challenge was to get a group of old dogs (who were used to showing up, getting out, and sprinting to the general location of the action) to somehow shackle their feet, and keep themselves in a fixed location (inside their response vehicle), so they could actually manage the event. On the surface, this may not sound like a very difficult task. In reality, it is no more difficult than getting a mule to play the piano.

Battalion Chief Harold was one of our most aerobic incident commanders. Sometimes, he would actually wait until his response sedan was fully stopped prior to launching himself out of it and into the fray.

We were several years into using our new system and Harold was still letting his feet lead him into bad command positions. He had just left a motivational one-on-one with the fire chief that was the result of a fire in a strip mall that went less than well. Harold was running the fire and had trouble getting reports from the engine company that he assigned to the rear of the building. This was the most recent siren song that sucked Harold out of his command post and into the world of physical action.

Instead of sitting in his rig and commanding the entire fire fight, Harold ended up in the back of the building swinging a sledge hammer, with his radio stuffed in his back pocket.

Harold's feet had positioned him in a place where he could no longer visualize the other eighty percent of the building (he was inside the occupancy where the fire had originated). Crews quickly knocked down the fire in Harold's little part of the world.

Harold's joy over a quick knockdown was quickly shattered when he walked out of the front door of the store he had helped to force entry into, only to visualize the heavy smoke showing from one end of the roof to the other. The fire had extended up the wall and into the large common attic that was shared by the other nine occupancies that made up the rest of the strip mall.

# The Anatomy and Physiology of Leadership

Harold knew that he would have to explain to his boss why his uncontrollable feet had caused the fire loss to quadruple for today's fire.

A week after Harold's latest fire-side chat with his boss, he had a life-changing event. It was of a spiritual magnitude and had a value that easily outweighed a million stern lectures. Such is the case when you see the white light, long dead acquaintances, and feel the touch of God's hand.

Harold had been dispatched to a fire in a flop house. When he arrived at the scene, fire was burning in several rooms on the second floor of a two-story YMCA-style apartment building.

A couple of engine companies had attack lines on the second floor and were actively fighting fire. A ladder company was opening up the roof over the fire to vent the smoke and heat out of the building. Everything was going well on Harold's arrival.

He was determined to take command of the event and stay in his sedan. However, he looked up and noticed a man standing in an open window on the second floor, waving his arms and yelling to be rescued. Smoke was rolling out of the top of the window opening.

Harold's feet told his brain to kiss their ass and forced Harold's hand to open the door. Before Harold knew it, his feet had taken his entire body to a ladder truck, and his arms and hands had taken possession of a 16-foot straight ladder. The feet were now transporting Harold up the ladder towards the open window to save the trapped man.

Many of you, not familiar with fire fighting operations (and a few that are), probably feel that Harold's current actions are not only justified, but an absolute requirement in this given situation.

The first time I heard this story was from a newspaper reporter who enjoyed "slumming" in the fire station to which I was assigned. He was aghast that the fire chief took issue with Harold's "manage-on-the-run" style. Like most everything else in this reporter's life, he was also wrong about this issue.

Physical action is a biological and emotional response to stress. It takes a combination of training, application, and discipline to do the right thing; this includes taking the correct action. Harold's role was no longer to get out and physically immerse himself in the work; it was to manage getting the work done. Harold's position required a mouth for talking, ears for listening, and an ass to sit on, while

*Foot*

# The Anatomy and Physiology of Leadership

he did it. The chief's (i.e., IC's) job is to command--when they stop doing that, no one is in charge, and things quickly spiral out of control. Harold's feet always doubled the fire damage. Now they were about to get him killed.

After Harold's body expertly placed the ladder in the window, he climbed the ladder and deposited himself into the smoke-filled room. If Harold's ears had been listening to the tactical radio channel, they would have heard that an engine company had already rescued the room's occupant and that he was safely outside.

Harold stumbled around the small room finding no one. Harold's brain reasoned that the man had left the room and headed down the hallway to the stairs. As Harold opened the door and stepped into the hallway, which was filled from the floor to ceiling with acrid and toxic brown smoke, he heard the door close behind him.

As luck would have it, the door was locked and Harold was now stranded on the second floor, fifty feet from the exits. This wouldn't have been a major set back if Harold was part of an engine or ladder crew, wearing turnouts and an SCBA, with the protection of a charged hose line. All the protection Harold had was his shiny gold badge, which told the world that he outranked everyone else on the scene (except the fire). The trouble was it didn't flow any water or deliver any fresh air.

He collapsed thirty feet from the stairs--just another clinically dead guy lying in the hall.

Attack crews had a handle on the fire. Search crews had cleared the second floor and were heading down the hallway and out of the building, when they literally tripped over Harold. Visibility was still very poor, and they assumed they were pulling an unconscious resident out of the building. It wasn't until they got half way down the stairs that they realized they had the chief.

Once Harold was safely out of the building, crews forced fresh oxygen into his lungs, and brought him back from the dance with the dead.

Harold was sitting on the curb, looking like the Second World War when his boss sat down beside him, and asked if he was all right. Despite the pounding headache, Harold smiled and nodded. The reign of Harold's feet was finally over.

# The Anatomy and Physiology of Leadership

## Heart

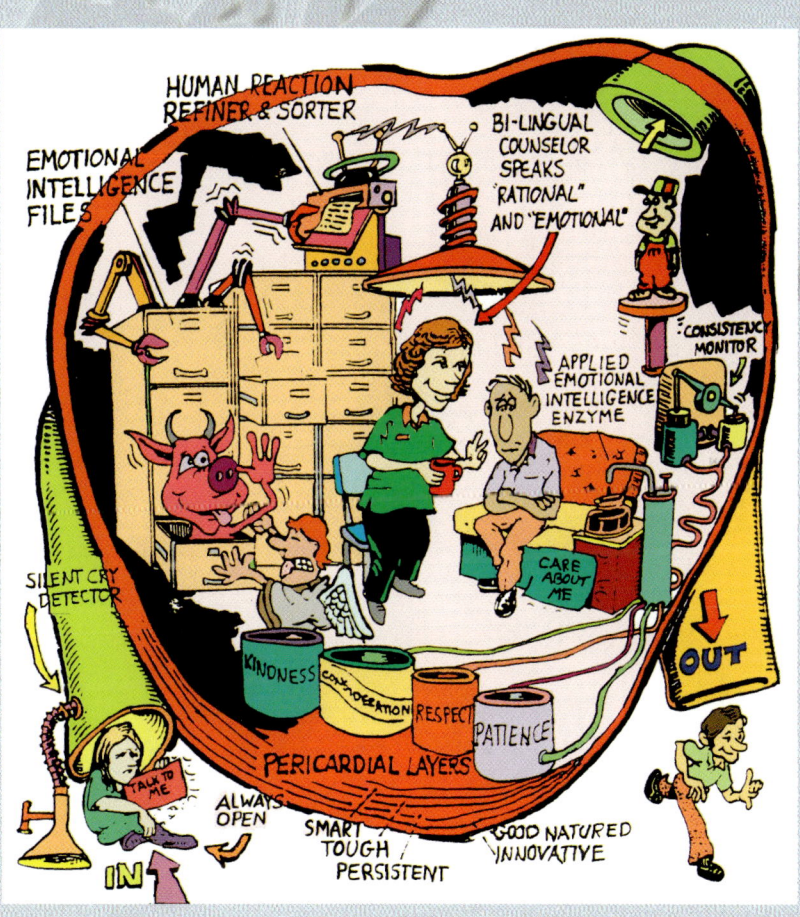

# The Anatomy and Physiology of Leadership

# The Anatomy and Physiology of Leadership

# Heart

## Basic Leadership Capability

Down at the Ajax Machine Shop, they generally promote bosses because they are whiz-bang drill press operators (you probably wouldn't promote lousy drill press operators). When this promotion occurs, the new boss takes off their coveralls, gets a snazzy new boss shirt, with their name and the Ajax logo on it. Along with the new shirt comes the responsibility for a dozen drill presses (that they really understand), and twelve drill press operators (who are almost immediately baffling to them). The new boss quickly discovers that drill presses don't have feelings, seldom talk back, and never call in sick because their families have the flu--simply, human relations is quite different from drill-press relations.

The new boss realizes (if they survive as a new boss) that the most critical part of effective leadership involves dealing with the nonrational, emotional-based feelings of the humans that do the work of the enterprise. They also discover (the quicker the better) that effective bosses must use their heart in very different and special ways, simply because workers are humans (not machines). Many times we humans mostly do stuff, not because of what we know, but because of how we feel. Bosses also quickly learn that being a day-to-day boss has a special relationship with how their workers get through the day-- most of this relationship is based on the personal behavior of the boss.

Our heart is where our emotions live. It is the critical care center (i.e., intensive care unit) of our other A & P parts and is what makes leaders human. Our emotions create a natural balance with the intellectual and rational capabilities of our brain. We can (as bosses) refine and improve (actually train) our emotional literacy to better understand how our feelings influence our

# The Anatomy and Physiology of Leadership

## Heart (cont.)

leadership reactions to human situations. Understanding and refining these human reactions and capabilities increase our emotional intelligence.

The effective use of this increased/improved emotional intelligence creates the capability to lead in a human way that reflects kindness, consideration, respect, and patience. This approach becomes the foundation for the boss/worker relationship and leaders who consistently reflect these characteristics are regarded simply as being nice (big deal). Experienced leaders who are consistently effective balance nice with other personal characteristics like smart, tough, persistent, accessible, good natured, innovative, etc.

Operating from a foundation of "nice" causes such bosses to always go back (default) from wherever they are to those basic (nice) behaviors. A smart person said, "The three most important things to remember are kindness, kindness, and kindness." Such effective leaders also realize the heart has great versatility that can create a full range of powerful emotions, which can go from warm and positive to cold and dark.

Leaders must understand that as they rise in the system, they typically become subject to a screwy paradox--they must more and more understand, relate to, and service the emotional needs of others, while they receive less and less emotional support themselves. Simply, it comes with the "boss territory" because we are all expected to become more emotionally self-sufficient as we move up in the organization.

While this expectation is a reality, it does not represent in any way the real emotional needs of bosses. Bosses are just humans in promoted positions--they have all the same body parts (needs) as the workers. Leaders become more effective as they control and manage their own dark human emotions such as hatred,

# The Anatomy and Physiology of Leadership

## Heart (cont.)

deep covert fear, rage, jealousy, revenge, lust, and stupid ego stuff. Their own heart becomes "smarter" and learns to expect, identify, not be surprised by, understand, deal with, and react to those characteristics in others.

Dealing with these natural human feelings produces an increased level of emotional literacy which also creates the understanding that our feelings and emotions (heart) speak one language, and our rational/intellectual side (brain) speaks another. Simply, it is futile to try to communicate in rational terms with someone who is in an emotional state... and vice versa.

Effective leaders must become fluent in each language (rational/emotional) and then develop an effective interface between the two. Simply, to be effective, bosses must become "bilingual." This two-language capability (inter-operability) becomes useful in both understanding ourselves and in effectively dealing with others.

Like other human components, our heart is highly vulnerable to injury and can take a hit that can produce damage ranging from a minor bruise to a major fracture. Other body parts get scuffed up physically. The heart gets beaten up emotionally... emotional injury can hurt a lot more, for a longer period of time, and is harder to both forget and heal. Major emotional injury can be the most debilitating, serious, and sometimes unresolvable setback a human can sustain.

Regular medical damage control techniques used on other body-part injuries do not apply to the repair of a broken heart. Unattended and untreated broken hearts will eventually cause emotional (and sometimes physical) death. Developing a strong heart with a resilient "bounce back" factor becomes a

# The Anatomy and Physiology of Leadership

## Heart (cont.)

major human survival capability. Actually, it is difficult to go back so true resiliency results from "bouncing forward"... let go, get over it, and develop a new normal.

We generally learn the most from tough times. When everything is okay, we just naturally coast along and enjoy the comfy view. When we start getting scuffed up, we wake up and start paying attention to whatever is causing the scuffs. A lot of times, these experiences produce the hard lessons that build emotional muscles. The problem with bouncing back to where we were before is that we missed the lesson and must keep making the same flub until we learn and get past that mistake (and get on to the new normal).

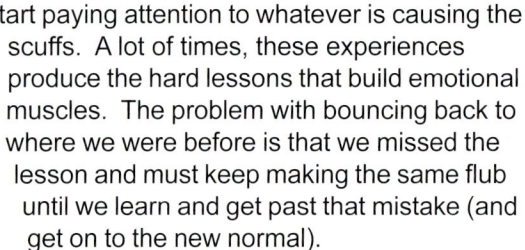

Such coronary strength is the result of actively understanding the affairs of the heart, training it to be strong and smart, and then using, not sheltering our emotions, and developing the capability to effectively recover from the tough stuff that life just naturally inflicts on us. This learning, recovering, getting emotionally smarter, and then moving on is what "bouncing forward" really means.

The workplace necessarily becomes a big-time emotional environment that can leave either a major + or - mark on the workers. Based on that reality, leaders and bosses have a major responsibility to strengthen and protect the hearts of workers by consistently applying positive, sensible, humane, and progressive *everyday* management techniques.

Managing in such an effective way produces a "boomerang" effect on the heart health of leaders... simply, you get what you give. Smart bosses quickly learn that they eventually get back what they give--and they will also eventually lose what they selfishly hoard for themselves.

# The Anatomy and Physiology of Leadership

## Heart (cont.)

### Rules of Engagement

■ Refine how you use your emotions for understanding and relating to other humans (refine = study, understand, receive info, process, and decide on how to act... over and over, and over, and over, etc.).

■ You must become emotionally literate:

- Heart is what makes you human.
- Only the heart can produce emotional logic.
- Emotions can only do emotional stuff (don't think with your heart/feel with your brain).
- You naturally have happy/sad/dark emotions.
- Emotional action plan and cardiac damage control:
    - happy--remember/enjoy
    - sad--process/recover (move on)
    - dark--understand/control/unload
      (Batman was a "dark" hero).

■ Heart directs everyone to emotionally decide right/wrong for themselves; right/wrong = important things in life.

■ DFR--doesn't feel right.

■ Increase your vocabulary--become bilingual... learn to speak and balance the correct language to match the situation:

- Speak emotional lingo in emotional situations.
- Speak rational lingo in rational situations.

# The Anatomy and Physiology of Leadership

## Heart (cont.)

- Understand the capabilities/limitations of your emotions in dynamic, real-life leadership situations.

- Balance your emotions--don't make decisions just on what your heart says--check it out with other body parts (brain first).

- Maintain an effective cardiac consistency: Not too hard/not too soft.

- Understand and remember that leadership is mostly about people:

  - They are human.
  - They mostly do what they want, based on how they feel.
  - Everyone wants to know what's going on and to have a "piece of the action."
  - They mostly respond to how you (as a leader) feel--mostly how you care about them.

- Apply protection for your heart:

  - Wear your "emotional protective gear."
  - Don't fight out of your weight class.
  - Pay attention.
  - Sometimes get "emotional body guards."
  - Get emotional first aid when you need it (quickly).

# The Anatomy and Physiology of Leadership

## Heart (cont.)

- Consider that every person has their own personal (emotional) billboard that is always flashing:

  - Pay attention to me/appreciate me.
  - Be nice to me... don't rain on my parade.
  - Listen to me.
  - Care about me.
  - Don't control me... let me try it, learn, and then help me.
  - Talk directly to me... in terms I understand.
  - Show me respect... in my "language."
  - Help me gain control of my career (and myself).
  - Don't waste my time.
  - Be honest with me.
  - Make me feel important.
  - Let me create my own success--I'll pay you back by supporting your success.
  - Don't disqualify my problem as an nonauthentic problem ("minimizing").
  - Empathize (don't sympathize).
  - Make me look good.
  - Forgive me when I screw up.

- Be very careful when dealing with feelings--we can recall only part of what we read and hear, but we remember 100% of what we feel.

# The Anatomy and Physiology of Leadership

## Heart (cont.)

- Understand how powerful "liking" is:

  - No one wants to be controlled by anyone they feel does not like them.
  - It is too expensive for a leader to "not like" someone (not liking causes us to do really dumb stuff).
  - The natural reaction to not being liked is to not like back (more stupid stuff) (pretty soon stupid vs. stupid = I'll see your idiot and raise you an imbecile).
  - When boss mixes not liking with formal power... lots of pain, everybody loses.

- Only the heart can hear a silent cry.

- BE NICE... avoid being un-nice.

- Understand and control your own personal billboard. Know your own emotional "buttons" or "devils"--be careful of showing your buttons... someone may push them.

# The Anatomy and Physiology of Leadership

## Heart

Being a firefighter is not for the weak of heart. Firefighters are around-the-clock participants in the full spectrum of life. We deliver babies into the world, and ours are the final faces many of our customers see as they depart this earthly domain. Our day is filled with tragedy, drama, comedy, kindness, and every other form of human emotion. Some days our shift feels like twenty-four hours of the *Oprah* show.

It is not easy to deliver emergency service to people suffering from physical and emotional trauma. I have noticed that the people most skilled and proficient at treating the sick and injured are very clinical. They perform like mechanics who work on human bodies instead of mechanical machinery. Each patient becomes a set of biological problems to be fixed.

Becoming emotional does no one any good. When the world is falling down around them, the last group our customers want (or need) coming to their rescue are a bunch of hypersensitive granola eaters. Swift, effective, and immediate action requires focus and concentration. Both of these attributes are tough to maintain when you are sobbing.

We are not robots and must somehow balance being skilled technicians with the very human effect that our work has on us. There is no easy way to comfort someone who has lost all of their earthly possessions because their home has just burned down, or console parents who have just lost a child. Some days life just flat-ass sucks, and there's nothing you can do about it.

In a city of over a million people, these kinds of devastating, life-altering events will happen to dozens of people on a daily basis.

Twenty years ago, the Phoenix Fire Department enlisted a group of mental health professionals to help us more effectively support our customers, who had just had the worst day of their lives, and to offer services to our firefighters who were having personal issues with some of the more disturbing calls they went on. We can bandage wounds, splint fractured bones, extinguish burning property, but we can't fix a broken heart (yours or ours-- only time can do that).

The crisis counselors I have worked with are caring, honest, and altruistic individuals. For the most part, they are all volunteers and feel it is their duty to help their fellow human beings.

Rank and file, street firefighters love these folks. They show up at the scene, minutes behind the initial-arriving units, and attend to the short-term physical and emotional needs of the customer and their loved ones. This allows firefighters to focus their efforts on mitigating the emergency.

# The Anatomy and Physiology of Leadership

## Heart

There are some things that people shouldn't have to see. Unfortunately, the nature of our job exposes us to life's horrors all too often. You know it's a bad day when seasoned firefighters, emergency-room doctors and nurses, and crisis counselors tap out after seeing some of the things behind life's little curtain.

I have a friend who regularly wades through the landscape of human pain and emotional suffering; his large heart seemingly bulletproof against tragedy. His name is Father Carl, the Phoenix Fire Department Chaplain, and he is quite possibly one of the least ecclesiastical people on the planet.

He is just a nice man who makes a very human connection with the people he comes into contact with. He deals with hundreds of families every year who have lost loved ones from natural causes, fire, suicide, drowning, violent crime, and all of the other ways we die, but Carl always shows up with tasty ice cream treats when he visits fire stations.

I have worked alongside firefighters who didn't seem to be bothered by any of this stuff. They respond on calls where other human beings have been torn in half, incinerated, decapitated--the full gamut of grizzly endings one can imagine, and it doesn't appear to faze them in the slightest.

It's a strange thing to see a guy have a tizzy fit because a spoon got tossed in the fork tray of the silverware drawer at the fire station, only to watch him go out and deal with death and mayhem like it was a no bigger deal than overcooked eggs.

It can be tricky trying to read other people's hearts. Some days the heart and actions of your fellow crew members are more mysterious than the hand of death.

Pete parked Engine 58 at an angle to protect the patient and his crew from southbound traffic. They had just pulled up on a car-pedestrian accident on the far west end of Phoenix. The roadway they were working on was bordered on both sides by large fields of corn. All the migrant workers had left their work and were hypnotized by the carnage in the middle of the road. Several police cars had arrived and the cops were now directing traffic and searching for witnesses to the accident. A family of workers was crossing the road when a car traveling more than 50 mph hit their young son.

One of the constants of our work is we rarely know what events led up to our arrival. Why was the family crossing the street in the first place? Did the boy drop something in the street and go back to get it, or did the family just misjudge the speed of the approaching

# The Anatomy and Physiology of Leadership

traffic. A mother, father, and their young son started across the road and now one of them was dead.

I was a minute away when Engine 58's captain reported that he had a 901-H (dead person) and cancelled the balance of the assignment (helicopter, ambulance, second paramedic engine, the battalion chief and me), and requested Father Carl. I was close, so I continued to the scene to see what was up.

There is something surreal about seeing a body in the middle of the road covered with a blue, disposable EMS blanket. It really is a sad sight. I met up with the captain of Engine 58. He said that the boy was obviously dead, and he was going to stay with the family until Father Carl showed up.

One of his firefighters was fluent in Spanish and was presently dealing with the parents of the dead boy. All the firefighters on the scene had seen more than their share of death. Still, they felt horrible.

I broke the silence of our private moment, when I asked him what was up with all of the crows in the middle of the road, one hundred feet or so from the scene of the accident.

I was informed, "That's where the kid was initially hit by the car. He was thrown to where he's lying now. As far as the birds, I suppose the crows got tired of just eating corn."

It seemed like the perfect cue for the Chaplin's entrance to the scene and my exit.

The crew of Engine 58 is very good at what they do. On a purely task level, Pete the engineer is probably the most proficient at his job. Engineers, who operate pumpers, have the responsibility of always getting their crew water at the scene of structure fires.

In most cases, this is accomplished by stopping at a fire hydrant close to the scene and dropping off a firefighter to make the hydrant hook up. For a variety of reasons engines don't always take the time to stop at a fire hydrant, opting instead to go directly to the scene of the fire and commence fire attack.

This places the engineer in a very precarious position. The engineer has to set their rig up to pump, charge their crew's attack line with the proper water flow and pressure, and then hope that they can find a water source before the crew empties the 500 gallons of water that is carried in the water tank on the rig. Pete seems to magically produce a never-ending supply of water for his crew; they have never run out of water half way through a fire fight.

*Heart*

# *The Anatomy and Physiology of Leadership*

# Heart

Pete is also an excellent driver; he has never had an accident. He keeps his truck very clean. He is also a master mechanic.

One day, Engine 58 was responding to a call when the steering wheel mysteriously came off of the steering column. Many drivers would have panicked going forty-five miles an hour with lights and siren without the aid of steering. Pete never even blinked. He got the truck slowed down, managed to get the wheel back on the column, and finished responding to the call. While Pete is as close to technical perfection in the engineer's position as possible, he is also widely regarded as being a one-way prick.

Pete has never been accused of being big hearted. It is impossible to spend more than a couple hours around him without hearing unsolicited whining about the latest injustice he has had to live through.

It all boils down to Perfect Pete having to coexist with highly fallible humans; this includes family, friends, and as far as I can tell, every other anonymous person on the planet earth. After brief exposure, it is pretty easy to come to the conclusion that Pete's heart beats only for him.

In the little world that involves managing and supervising Pete, life is pretty simple--he shows up to work on time, does his job (as well as anyone else in the world), and keeps his comments to himself when he is out in public (he's not stupid). Every now and then, when you've had enough, you tell him to shut up and he settles down, becoming tolerable for another month.

Father Carl was making one of his routine station visits a couple weeks after the two of us shook hands on the side of a road that contained the dead boy. As usual, he showed up with a sack full of extra special ice cream treats (Dove Bars this time).

We were catching up on the latest gossip while trying to eat ice cream before it melted, when I asked how things went with our last encounter with the dead.

He told me, "The family's doing as well as can be expected. The thing I helped them with was getting the body transported to Mexico, so he could be buried in the family plot."

I said, "It seems to me that that would cost more than migrant workers could afford." Father Carl replied, "I have a fund for those

# The Anatomy and Physiology of Leadership

kinds of expenses, and offered to help, but the family said they could only take charity from the fire department one time, and they had enough money to get their son back home."

I asked, "Who from the fire department gave them that kind of money?" Father Carl said, "The mother told me that the Bombero (Spanish for firefighter) that drove the truck said he was very sorry for her loss and that they couldn't do anything to save her boy's life. Then before he got on the truck to leave, he walked back and gave her six-hundred dollars."

Our conversation went on for another couple of minutes, but I was preoccupied with the revelation. The money part didn't confuse me. Pete wasn't shy about hard work and had built up a very lucrative side business. It wasn't uncommon for him to walk around with a wad of bills in his pocket. What was puzzling me was the most coldhearted guy on the rig pressed hundreds of dollars into a stranger's hand. It was the nicest thing one person did for another on that day in a city of over one million people. The mysterious way the heart reacts is one of life's delicious little surprises.

# The Anatomy and Physiology of Leadership

*Heart*

# The Anatomy and Physiology of Leadership

# Body

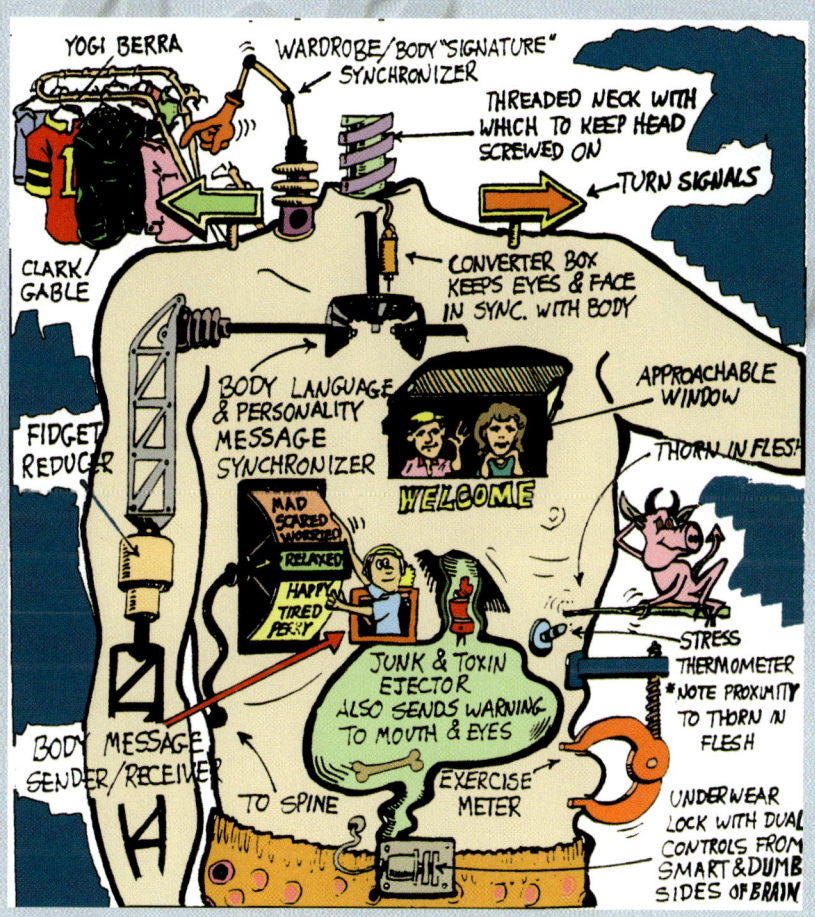

# The Anatomy and Physiology of Leadership

*Body*

# The Anatomy and Physiology of Leadership

# Body

## Basic Leadership Capability

The body serves as the personal A & P superstructure and physically becomes the biggest part of our individual "signature." That signature has the capability to create and send along highly influential leadership messages to others. This communications process is commonly known as body language. This is a separate A & P language that communicates in its own special way, has its own meaning and fluency, and must be effectively connected with other rational/emotional messages.

If the brain/heart/body messages are not in sync, the leader sends out confusing mixed-message signals that can create unwanted reactions in others.

Our body language is highly versatile and can quickly send messages like being happy, mad, scared, relaxed, worried, disgusted, impatient, bored, aggressive, sad, perky, droopy, tired, energetic, etc. The versatility of these body language messages makes them highly adaptable to a variety of different situations. Effective leaders realize the message each body (language) mode sends, and they learn to control how their body (language) looks to others.

Everyone comes from the factory with a natural style ("signature") that matches their personal profile. It's probably a pretty

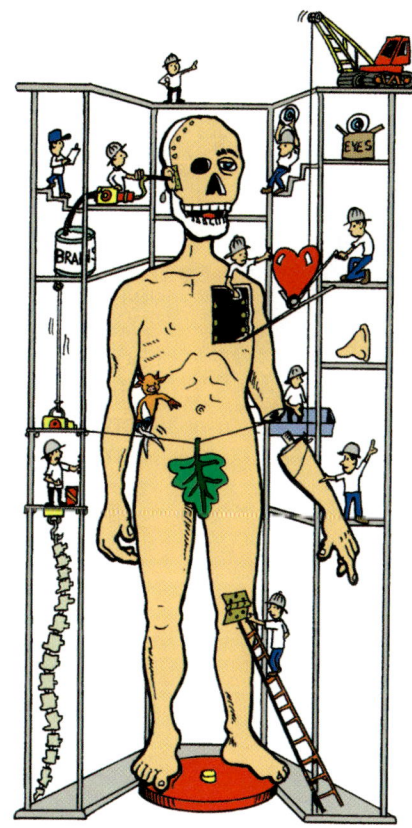

# The Anatomy and Physiology of Leadership

## Body (cont.)

unnatural act to try to make Yogi Berra look like Clark Gable (or vice versa). Leaders should study their own natural features (body type) and develop the inclinations and ability to take advantage of their positive personal characteristics. They should minimize the way their body characteristics can create a negative effect (for example, a big, tall, tough-looking body can be scary to others... must "get on the other person's level," and develop a more relaxed posture to send a "softer" message).

As leaders better understand their physical profile, they can then leverage their body profile into sending a strategic and effective message to different people and situations.

Body language has the same self/other characteristics as the other A & P parts... simply, the more we study and practice sending effective body messages ourselves, the better we become at reading, receiving, and reacting to body-language messages from others. The body is a person's primary pleasure site (amount/intensity).

The natural inclination for the body to feel good is a powerful force in human affairs. The brain must continually monitor and control the short-term pleasures that can cause the body long-term pain (and damage)... stuff like drugs, booze, smoking, excessive/wrong food, stress, etc. It's difficult to stop using/doing the pleasure stuff that hurts our body (simply) because it feels so good in the beginning. Typically people don't listen to warnings until it starts to hurt. Most of us disregard the standard issue advice/warnings (from parents, elders, advisors, old bosses, etc... "don't touch it; it's hot") and we must live through the painful lessons that come with the pleasurable experiences for ourselves.

How the lifestyle process turns out is pretty simple--if we learn the lessons early, we survive; if we don't get it until later (or never) and we continue the body abuse activity, the junk (from that activity) will eventually croak us.

# The Anatomy and Physiology of Leadership

## Body (cont.)

We must develop the understanding of a pretty basic natural law: There is a corresponding opposite pain scale that balances our "fun meter." Sooner or later a lot of what produces great (inappropriate, dumb, risky) fun on the feel-good side can also lead to an abrupt reversal that quickly ends up on the painful side. Simply for every yin, there is a yang... nothing is free (there is always a judgement day).

## Rules of Engagement

- Your body is your biggest part and can send the biggest message.

- Body language will always influence your message--keep it in sync with verbal, eye, and facial messages.

- Understand the huge number of possible body messages you can send. Consciously pick the message you want to send.

- Try to send positive, open-body message (in positive situations):
    - correct distance from people, places, and things--don't drive beyond "your headlights"
    - nonaggressive/nonthreatening
    - confident leadership stature
    - smooth actions
    - predictable... signal before you turn.

- Learn to observe, read, interpret, and react to body language--not to judge it.

# The Anatomy and Physiology of Leadership

## Body (cont.)

- Be aware of how all body parts influence (and "line up" with) body language.

- Be aware of cultural differences in body language "messages."

- Be careful of the other bodies your body hangs out with(!).

- Simple body-maintenance routine:

    - Tired--rest.
    - Hungry--eat.
    - Thirsty--drink.
    - Cold--banky.
    - Lonely--teddy.
    - Scared--buddy.

- Some body parts are better covered up (i.e., adequately clothed).

- Control your speed. Many times the fastest way to get to the middle and end is to slow down in the beginning (just a bit). Simply, do it right the first time.

# The Anatomy and Physiology of Leadership

## Body (cont.)

- Use open, approachable body language as a cue to lead others to relax and open up; strategically eliminate barriers/distractions:

    - Get out from behind stuff... desk, secretary, "guards."
    - Turn off phone and eliminate interruptions.
    - Pay attention; don't fidget--maintain eye contact.
    - Close door.
    - Make conversation partner comfortable.

- Pay attention: Lips can lie--body language doesn't.

- Do good body maintenance:

    - Eat smart.
    - Sleep/rest (lots of naps).
    - Exercise.
    - Unload stress--don't put junk in your body.
    - Bathe every day (with a rubber duck... security symbol).

- Remember, how you dress/groom creates a package that sends a big-time message; don't overpackage/underpackage--make how you look fit the situation.

- Be careful of becoming accustomed to and just living with something that hurts your body (living with the devil you know).

# The Anatomy and Physiology of Leadership

## Body

Firefighters are one of the few work forces that will physically place their bodies between the "customer" and great natural peril, in the course of doing their job. Our motto is if we can get our hands on you, we can save you. This motto is predicated with a single requirement of the customer--that you are savable when we get our mitts on you (i.e., dead no more than four to six minutes with all major body systems still intact, or at least fixable).

This has been a hallmark of our service for the past several thousand years. The only thing more symbolic than a gleaming red fire engine heading down the road is an infant child securely attached to its mother's breast.

The nature of our work has forged a very special relationship between our organizations and the communities we protect. Up until several decades ago, firefighters rated at the top of the public love and support food chain. Nowadays fire fighting plays a close second fiddle to the new owners of the number one spot--Paramedics.

In the pre-EMS days, we physically put our bodies between the customer and the fire. In the EMS era, we are saving our customer's bodies, and the bodies of their loved ones; this is a much more consistent, up close, and personal service.

Most people will not have their home or business burn down, limiting our customer base. On the other hand, most people will have, or be indirectly connected to, some type of medical emergency during their lifetime (in fact, many times life ends in some type of medical emergency).

Delivering EMS to the community causes us to go out and touch the people--much like the beloved Mother Theresa. Despite what televangelists think, there is no greater human thing that you can do for a person than save their life or the life of their loved ones. It doesn't take a roomful of rocket scientists to figure out why we are so well thought of.

It was no small feat for the fire service to jump into the EMS business. Almost overnight we went from exclusively fighting the menace of fire, which tends to be an extremely violent, exciting, and hazardous undertaking to caring for the sick and injured.

Having a group of manly men (not many women in the service back in those days) perform double duty as fighters and compassionate health care providers has been a long and winding road. Expanding our service delivery menu and providing EMS is the smartest thing fire departments have done since they figured out that water puts out fire.

# The Anatomy and Physiology of Leadership

It has cemented our place in society, added more flavor to our careers, and expanded our experiences as people. It has also proven itself to oftentimes be every bit as violent, exciting, and hazardous an undertaking, as structural fire fighting. It isn't always easy putting your body between the sick and injured and the rest of the world.

A wedding ceremony was taking place nearby. It was a traditional Catholic affair. The Padre said the mass; the bride was wrapped in a big, white puffy dress and the kids, in suits and dresses that were too big, threw rose petals.

The difference between this wedding and say one that was being thrown anywhere in the state of Iowa during the same hour was that most of the wedding guests wore baggy jeans, long-sleeved, starched denim work shirts, "do-rags," and left their sunglasses on during the church service.

The physical appearance of their bodies left no doubt about who they were. The ceremony ended with the bride crying real tears of joy, the groom's (tears) were tattoos.*

The after party was in full swing. Social gatherings of this magnitude are always advertised in advance and are well known by the community of neighbors, friends and, in this case, rival gangs with a score to settle.

* special street-gang murder symbol

A few of the major social organizations that didn't know this wedding and ensuing celebration were taking place on that blessed day were the Phoenix Police Department Maryvale Precinct and Phoenix Fire Station 44. They were about to receive a late invitation.

It was just after 11:00 p.m. and the crew of Engine 44 was finishing up with the dinner dishes. Swing shift cops were out and about, fighting crime.

The bride and groom had consumed enough Bud Light to kill a classroom full of fifth graders. The two-hundred plus wedding guests were doing their best to follow suit.

The three young men in a plain-looking sedan appeared to be quite sober as they drove down the street toward the happy party. They had stolen the car earlier that day and planned their route past the party, so the passenger side of the vehicle would be facing the house. This way the driver could focus on driving, and the two passengers could concentrate on shooting people.

I don't remember the specifics of what I was doing with my body when all of these events collided. I just know that I was at work, four miles up the road at Fire Station 25, when the lights came on, and the voices told us to go to a shooting with multiple victims, somewhere in Engine 44's first-due area.

# The Anatomy and Physiology of Leadership

# Body

My partner and I climbed into our battalion rig and headed out into the muzzle-flash filled night.

All of us use our bodies in some manner to do our jobs. This evening's work would involve firefighters using theirs to treat customers who suffered gunshot wounds. These incident scenes tend to be confusing, emotional, and oftentimes very hazardous places.

My job is to manage these kinds of events. Things go better when I keep my body in the rig, figure out what's going on, and use our department's space-age radio system to coordinate the activities of the various pieces of fire department equipment and personnel.

It is our preference that for calls involving violent crime law enforcement goes in first and secures the scene. The police have guns; we don't.

If the customers are still playing shoot 'em up, we (the fire department) have no business anywhere near the scene--it's a cop matter until they are reasonably certain no one will shoot the firefighters.

After the cops clear the scene, we march our bodies in and do our thing. Cops ought to stay out of burning buildings, and firefighters should avoid stumbling into the middle of gunfights.

Because the 9-1-1 caller reported that several people had been shot, the Alarm Room dispatched the call as a 2-1 medical. This put two paramedic engine companies, two ambulances (one happened to be staffed with paramedics), and a battalion chief (me) on the incident.

Engine 44 was the first unit to arrive on the scene. The crew staged a couple blocks east of the scene and reported to our Alarm Room (communication's center) that the scene was chaotic and that they would hold their position until PD was able to secure the incident site.

Police cars were driving into the scene at high rates of speed, while the partygoers were matching the cop's speed, driving away from the scene.

The scene itself was bedlam. Women with heavily made-up eyes cradled significant others who had taken rounds and cried for holy intervention from Jesus and the Virgin Mary.

None of us (from the fire department) were the slightest bit shocked or nervous over the current goings-on. We respond to these kinds of calls on at least a weekly basis. As sad as it is to say, this activity is a regular part of the landscape in big urban areas.

# The Anatomy and Physiology of Leadership

The first month I had been assigned to Battalion 3, I responded to and got to see ten people who had been shot to death (this didn't count the people who had been shot and survived). That works out to one a shift. The group of us had been to this rodeo more times than we cared to remember.

We share a couple of radio frequencies with the cops. I was still responding when the cops came over one of these channels and requested that a staged fire unit come into the scene to treat one of the "customers."

They said it just like that, because the police liked to tease us about our customer-centered approach in dealing with the public and our all-around, wholesome, good-guy image.

Engine 44 answered their request and asked them for specifics about the patient. PD directed Engine 44 to the front yard of the shooting gallery. When the crew of Engine 44 navigated their way through the mayhem, they found four people had been shot.

They requested that one of the staged ambulance crews come into the scene and assist them with treatment and transportation. At that point there were six or seven cops in the front yard and a few more in the house.

The senior members of the gang were finishing up an impromptu meeting in the backyard and were heading out front. All of them were mad and armed with semi-automatic handguns. The confusion out front was about to turn angry.

Engine 44's captain had requested more paramedic units and ambulances to be dispatched to the scene. Between his crew and the two ambulances, they were treating two of the four patients in the front yard.

One of the patients had been put on the back burner because the gunshot wound to his arm was deemed non-life threatening. The fourth patient was triaged the same priority for opposite reasons. He had been shot in the head, was not breathing, and had no pulse. His body was dead, and there was nothing anyone on this planet could do to make it otherwise.

Engine 44's captain hadn't been inside the house or backyard and assumed there were more patients than the four he currently had out front.

This was one of the rare instances where the mere bodily presence of police did not quell the situation. The cops had their hands full

# The Anatomy and Physiology of Leadership

and were hesitant to get into a shoot-out under the present circumstances, so they had switched to hand-to-hand combat with their customer base.

People were running, being tackled and shackled. There were not enough cops on the scene to take control. Fire crews out front were starting IVs, administering oxygen, and taking vital signs, when half a dozen or more gang members burst through the front door of the house into the informal treatment area.

They (gang members) had different triage protocols than the paramedics. Several members of the gang found their fallen comrade, who had been shot in the head. They were upset that he was not being treated, while victims of lesser status in their organizational hierarchy had garnered the attention of the paramedics.

Conversations carried on over the barrel of a gun tend to be very brief and one-sided. This one was no different--save my friend, or you die. The captain's decision was a no brainer. He assigned his paramedic and one of the ambulance crews to treat the brain-shot patient, who was quickly put on a gurney, placed in the back of an ambulance, and transported away from the scene.

A few seconds later, it seemed like it was raining cops. The air was thick with pepper spray and dozens of well-starched young men, and a few women, lay face down with their arms handcuffed behind their backs. The party was officially over.

We treated the few remaining patients, ascertained that all of our firefighters were okay and went available. On our way back to quarters, we got a message from our Dispatch Center to stop by Station 44.

We pulled into the back of the station. It had the look and charm of a Taco Bell fast food restaurant. An ambulance was parked behind the station; the two-firefighter ambo crew was cleaning blood and other body parts out of the patient compartment. It hadn't been fifteen minutes since they left the scene--certainly not enough time to transport the patient to the hospital and make it back to the station.

Firefighters assigned to ambulances are just starting their careers and tend to be shy around chief officers. The engineer paramedic assigned to Engine 44 was a ten-year veteran and was not the least bit intimidated by a chief; after all, he had just gotten to listen to someone holding a gun to his face.

I said hello and asked what was up. He repeated the story I heard less than twenty minutes ago from his captain.

# The Anatomy and Physiology of Leadership

I told him, "You guys went with the only option you had. A 9 millimeter outranks our triage system."

He responded, "Well thanks for saying so, but that's not why we called you. We kinda' have a situation we don't know how to handle."

The ambulance crew was looking very nervous and had increased their cleaning efforts. I had no clue why they needed me at their station or what situation they were having trouble dealing with. This was the same group that had calmly dealt with violent death from criminals just a few minutes ago.

I told them, "Why don't you just spit it out? It can't be that big a deal."

They replied, "Well we didn't have any choice in picking which patient we were going to treat and transport. We wrote off the guy we ended up with, until his buddies changed our minds. Once I got him in the back of the ambo, I figured we could work him until we reached the hospital. He wasn't breathing, so I had the firefighter bag him. As soon as he gave him the first blast of oxygen, the remaining half of his brain fell out of the large hole in the back of his head. Well, needless to say, any further resuscitation efforts would be futile."

I said, "I understand, he was dead when you guys loaded him in the back of the ambo."

They reported, "The problem we had is we don't transport obviously dead people to the hospital, and his friends would have shot us if we took him back to the scene."

I had a freaky vision of the ambo hanging a u-turn, backing into the maylay in the front yard, the rear doors flying open and a corpse rolling out of the back doors.

I told them, "You only have one choice when you put someone in the back of an ambo, you take them to the hospital. Does it really matter if they're dead or alive?"

One of the firefighters said, "I patched with our doc, and he told us to stop working the patient. He also wanted us to take the body back to the scene or to the morgue. We didn't know where the morgue was; we were stumped."

All of the sudden it occurred to me that the body wasn't in the back of the ambulance, and it hadn't been transported to the hospital.

I asked, "What did you guys do with the body?"

*Body*

# Body

They told me, "We wrapped it up in a salvage cover and put it over next to the mops. Do you think the coroner will come out here and pick it up? We tried calling but got their answering machine."

On the other side of the ambo was a long wash rack used for washing 50-foot long sections of fire hose. The end of the run, closest to the station, has a large grate that drains into the sewer. The mop rack was located next to this drain.

I walked over and looked at the body wrapped in a black plastic salvage cover. It was the first time I had seen a dead person stored behind a fire house. The crew had secured the plastic sheet to the body by wrapping duct tape around the neck, shoulders, waist, and feet.

I said, "Shit, I don't know what to do with it. Can't you guys drop it off at the hospital?"

The firefighter told me, "I called four of them. They all refused." I replied, "Let's call the cops. They'll know what to do; we leave them dead bodies all the time."

The cops were having a very active night and were not about to send officers out to screw around with a dead body that the fire department mistakenly had in their possession. I remember the sergeant telling me over the phone that the body was "still our customer," and we would have to hold on to it until the Coroner's Office could send someone out for it in the morning.

He gave me one final piece of advice, "Whatever you do, don't leave it outside or the dogs will get it, and then we will have a real problem on our hands."

It was after one in the morning and not knowing what else to do, we moved the body into the apparatus bay, next to the lawn mower. After looking at the new storage arrangement on the apparatus floor everyone was in total agreement that hospitals make better places to store the dead, until they can be picked up by the warm and fuzzy folks from the morgue.

Firefighters are unique people, and I wasn't the slightest bit shocked that none of the crew seemed to mind spending the night in the station with a corpse. My partner and I wished them luck and drove back to our quarters.

The next morning the oncoming C shifters showed up for work a few minutes before the coroner picked up the cargo, and wouldn't you know it, they acted like we had left them a dead body.

# The Anatomy and Physiology of Leadership

# Gut

# The Anatomy and Physiology of Leadership

*Gut*

# The Anatomy and Physiology of Leadership

# Gut

## Basic Leadership Capability

The gut becomes the storage site for a very strong set of leadership instincts that can provide very quick, useful information and direction. These gut instincts are the result of a leader's experience (study, practice, application, reflection), their individual personality, and their own cosmic belief system. This capability quietly (and naturally) develops as that person struggles through life and bumps up against the agony and ecstasy of the human condition. These reactions create a very personal A & P to evaluate what we can (and should) "get away with" and what we can't (or shouldn't) "get away with." This evaluation capability becomes a huge part of how we survive and prosper as we go through life. These are the instincts and intuitions that are buried the "deepest" in that person.

Gut feelings (like "butterflies" in your stomach) didn't "go to school" so they are loaded directly, stored in the "gut storage file" and then unloaded when a person, place, or thing connects to something in that storage file. They are directly programmed on the most unrefined and primitive level; therefore, gut messages have a short feedback loop... they are quick and generally not complex.

Simply, the gut doesn't have to go through the rigmarole (process) like the thinking and emotions do. An incoming snapshot of the outside person, place, or thing goes directly into the gut files, and those files quickly select a gut reaction along with a corresponding (i.e., matching) message and, bingo, that message goes directly to the brain (simple, huh?).

# The Anatomy and Physiology of Leadership

## Gut (cont.)

The gut, like the nose, is particularly useful in the beginning of a leadership event (when typically there is not a lot of information and not a lot of discretionary time) because it can produce an "okay/not okay--go/no go" message very quickly.

The more senses and levels the leader can simultaneously engage and integrate, the more effective they become. Leaders should develop an ongoing routine to access and acknowledge gut instincts, as a primitive but powerful reality check, and creatively combine gut stuff with other A & P components as an important part of the initial and ongoing evaluation, decision-making, and operational process.

Don't underestimate intestinal intelligence. The gut has the same number of neurotransmitters as the brain. While it is as smart as the brain, it just reflects its intelligence in a different way. It serves as the brain's alarm system. The gut quickly scans the environment, produces a quick reaction, and sends it to the noodle where it is received, processed, evaluated, and develops a decision on an appropriate reaction.

The process is most effective when the gut and brain work as tag-team partners. This partnership requires an unobstructed, direct connection between the two.

### Rules of Engagement

- Don't disregard or deny gut instincts... if it's there; it's there.

- Don't be gutless.

# The Anatomy and Physiology of Leadership

## Gut (cont.)

- Realize the gut doesn't have a lot of separate layers, stages, or confusing stuff to "unlearn," so it's very direct and goes right to the issue.

- The gut speaks a primitive language--can be the best for the basic, primitive parts of initial and ongoing situation evaluation/management.

- A "gut check" in initial situations can provide a useful warning/caution. Determine if the environment is safe/unsafe and if the basic beginning mode should be offensive or defensive.

- When you get a gut alarm, stay out of the hazard zone, and procrastinate until you can do further checks with other body parts (be very careful of *all* types of possible secondary "explosions").

- Gut check is an important piece (gun behind the door) of basic leadership risk management.

- During ongoing situation management, gut instincts should continue to run and be mixed with and validated by other body parts.

- Listen to your "JDLR" (just doesn't look right) radar/instinct.

- Smart leaders continue to refine the accuracy, memory, and recall of their gut capabilities.

# The Anatomy and Physiology of Leadership

# Gut

Human beings are amazing machines. The most powerful computers ever built can only hope to play to a draw when competing against a human master in the game of chess.

Animals are better at any physical activity than humans. They can run faster, jump higher, see in the dark, and drag more weight.

This is insignificant when you measure it against making music, creating art, building the pyramids, cooking the perfect chili dog, and the invention of air conditioning.

We have used the sum of our parts to create civilization. This can leave a person tired at the end of the day. It doesn't matter if it's mowing the grass, running a marathon, writing articles, or having to think. Any constant activity will eventually exhaust a person.

An individual who spends all day designing a new airplane will be every bit as worn out as the people who spend all day building it, flying it, or repairing it (and in this case, the people who have to ride in the thing).

Our brains have evolved work/rest cycles, so we don't fall over unconscious halfway through the day.

We all go through large parts of our day on autopilot. We become so familiar and adept at doing repetitive tasks that we unconsciously do them while we think about other things.

Who hasn't second guessed whether or not they locked their front door as they pull out of the driveway? Don't bother going back to check, it's locked. Our brains are idling along until some kind of external stimulus taps our shoulder and brings us back into the physical world of the here and now.

Even during periods of exceptional monotony and boredom, our senses are pumping thousands of minute pieces of subliminal information to our brain. Each of these nuggets may seem innocuous when taken separately, but sometimes added together, they take on a whole new meaning.

When our brain processes a deeper meaning than what our individual senses are feeding it, we give the credit to our "gut." Our noses may detect that something isn't right, but we don't take action until all of the little, unconscious pieces of information hit our gut.

This is true for all animals. Watch any nature show that features big cats. The pretty little deer, zebra, and other cat-food creatures merrily go about their grazing. They stop and raise their noses in the air because they sense something is amiss. These animals will all stand perfectly still, up until the time their

## The Anatomy and Physiology of Leadership

# Gut

gut tells them to run. The nose smells danger; the gut makes Bambi move.

A gut feeling is always worth more than a casual observation. People who ignore their gut feelings end up broke, divorced, catching communicable diseases, and dead. The intuitive pay attention to the small details around them, listen to their gut, and then act.

Only xenophobes, the incompetent, and mentally ill go full-speed ahead when their gut tells them that something doesn't "feel right." Sometimes you just know when something really bad is about to happen.

My partner, Lynn, and I were taking our time heading to the "smell of electrical" at an apartment complex just south, on the freeway. Between the two of us, we had been on thousands of these types of "bells and smells" calls.

In most cases when someone smells some new, unidentifiable smell and calls 9-1-1, it ends up being a fluorescent light ballast, barbecue, sewer gas, something dead, or a figment of the caller's imagination.

Our response on this latest olfactory expedition started off a little differently. An engine company had been dispatched as a single unit and filled out the response (i.e., called for more units) because the crew knew something a little more serious than a week-old fart was producing the odor they were tracking.

We pulled into one of the parking lots of the large apartment complex and settled into to a spot that offered us a view of the east end of the complex. The property was made up of three-dozen separate buildings. The buildings were two-story, and each one of them contained eight separate apartments.

We had a nice view of the utilities building. It was several thousand square feet, made out of large reinforced concreted block, with a flat roof. It held the hot water boilers and big pieces of electrical equipment that distributed power to the separate apartment buildings.

It was lunchtime and foot traffic was pretty minimal, mostly momacitas with their kiddies (or meehos). We didn't transfer command because we didn't expect the event to escalate beyond the requirements of one or two engine companies. Engine 18 had been on the scene for five minutes, were hot on the trail of the elusive smell in the seven-acre apartment complex, and were doing a lovely job commanding the event.

My gut woke up when Engine 18 called us over the radio and asked if we would take

# The Anatomy and Physiology of Leadership

## Gut

command from them. They had just run across a fifty-foot long section of the ground that had them stumped. They reported that the dirt appeared to be smoking.

Lynn obliged and took command, asking them if something buried appeared to be on fire. Engine 18 came back and said, "No. It looks like the dirt itself is on fire."

Dirt isn't supposed to burn. If you pour gasoline on dirt and set it ablaze, the gas will burn and the dirt will remain. Our collective guts were wide awake.

Engine 18 had located the probable source of our noonday visit. An underground trenching crew was running cable into the apartment complex. They were using a "weasel" to run the below-grade trenching. This is a device that bores beneath the surface, avoiding the labor, time, expense, and mess of having to dig traditional ditches.

The crew had mistakenly bored through some underground electrical lines. Electricity is hot enough to burn dirt. Lynn requested that the power company immediately respond to the scene.

A minute later, I determined that requesting the power company was a stroke of genius when half a dozen large electrical boxes throughout the apartment complex began pumping out nasty black smoke.

The fire department requests the power company a minimum of eight or nine times a day. They generally show up within twenty to thirty minutes.

Our Alarm Room came back and let us know that the power company was really busy, and they would try to send someone within the next hour.

Lynn answered, "Coulter Command to Alarm… give me the balance of a first alarm haz-mat, be advised that we are going to begin evacuating this 300-hundred unit apartment complex, and we want the power company here right now."

I was both proud and sad that Lynn didn't use a four-letter word when describing the urgency of getting the electrical professionals to the scene. My heart said do it, but my gut thought it was better he hadn't.

Every electrical device in sight was issuing smoke, and Engine 18 was now reporting that the long stretch of dirt had ceased smoking and was actually flaming.

We focused all of our efforts on getting everyone evacuated from the large complex. Three engine companies were parked on the west side of incident site. Their crews were going from apartment to apartment and ushering the occupants out of harm's way.

# The Anatomy and Physiology of Leadership

We were the only fire department unit on the east side of the apartment complex. Lynn and I are managers. We show up at the scene of escalating events and coordinate what's going on. We make it a rule never to get out of our rig/command post. Leaving the confines and protection of a vehicle subjects you to all of the open air distractions one normally finds at the scene of structure fires and other chaotic and dangerous events.

I sat and watched in loathing disgust as one of the residents walked over to the buzzing utility building. Not two minutes earlier did I leave the sanctity of the command post to tell this person to run for her life. Now she was jabbering into her cell phone and investigating the force that was humming and causing the hair to stand up on the back of your neck. My gut was screaming that this event had "bad ending" written all over it.

Power panels throughout the complex were erupting in flame. The scene in front of us caused Lynn's sixth sense to stop talking into the radio and tell me, "If you can't get that stupid woman to get away from that building within the next minute or so, she's going to get to talk to God."

I went to the back of our rig and got out a roll of red, hazard tape. This color tape is used to alert firefighters that under no circumstance are they to cross its boundary. We used it to identify the location of large holes, the presence of deadly substances, and to restrict access around a building that's getting ready to fall over. Red tape means no-man's land.

In this case, I was using it to keep people away from a building about to be bathed in 100,000 volts of electricity (at least that's what my gut was telling me). As I placed the red tape around the general area of the building, I could see through an open door that a series of electrical panels inside the utility room were glowing red.

I conveyed to the misguided tenant that she had to leave. The woman was in her mid thirties, wore a black tube top that showed off her stretch-mark covered gut and green polyester Capri pants. There was confusion in her eyes as she said, "Que?" I responded the only Spanish word I knew appropriate for the circumstances, "Vamanos." She flipped me the bird, turned around and walked off.

I returned to the relative safety and calm of the command post. As I sat and listened to the radio traffic describing the evacuation process and the status of everything electrical, I wasn't surprised to see my new friend turnaround and return to the energized building. I took a few steps out of the rig and threw rocks at the idiot. She left for good.

*Gut*

# The Anatomy and Physiology of Leadership

## Gut

Our on-duty hazmat expert arrived at the scene and made his way to the command post. I filled him in on what we knew while waiting for the rest of his posse of hazmat heads to show up.

Neither one of us had a good feeling about the situation. This point was validated when one of the electrical panels in the utility room exploded and sent a shower of fireworks through the doorway of the building (where my Chiquita Princess had been standing a mere three minutes ago).

The explosion sounded like artillery going off. The loud thud, which could be felt in the gut and the bones, was followed by the unmistakable sound of arcing electricity. The power company troubleshooter couldn't have picked a better time to show up.

This man was every bit of six foot six and weighed well over three-hundred pounds. He was not fat; he was plain-ass big. His head may have been too large to fit in a grocery bag.

The hazmat guy and I regurgitated the current situation to him. There was a very big electrical box adjacent to the doomed utility building. Beyond it, you could see smoke coming from the electrical panels on all of the apartment buildings rising above the roof line. He started to go under the red tape toward the power box.

I stopped him and asked, "Where are you going." He replied, "I'm going over there to look inside that power box." I said, "I don't think that's a very good idea."

He looked down at me with a look that was equal parts surprise and contempt. He didn't seem like the kind of person that explained himself very often. He asked, "Are you telling me how to do my job?"

I replied, "I wouldn't dream of telling you how to do your job, just like I won't tell the medics how to do their job when your electricity blows that building, and you with it, all the way to Tucson."

He growled, "Listen buddy, I've been doing this a long time. If I don't go over and look into that box, a lot more than that building might explode. Are you going to keep me from doing my job?"

I looked to my hazmat expert and asked, "What do you think?" My expert replied, "Could be dangerous." Some days you can't even get bad help.

I told the power ranger, "Partner, I won't stop you, but I strongly urge you to figure out a plan B."

With that he ducked under the tape and went over and unlocked the large electrical cabinet.

# The Anatomy and Physiology of Leadership

I told our hazmat guru not to cross the tape under any circumstances and keep his eye out for an angry Hispanic woman before I jumped back into the command post with my command partner.

Electrical man must not have liked what he saw inside the electrical box. He slammed the door, ducked under the red tape, and ran back to his truck.

I watched as he fished a long pole with some type of contraption on the end of it out of the bed of his pickup. It looked like a device for trimming trees.

Fire companies in the apartment complex radioed that they had the entire complex evacuated. Within a minute of arriving at the scene, it felt like someone drilled a hole in the tops of our heads and had been slowly pouring dread into the blow hole. We were almost filled all the way up. I was sick of listening to my gut.

I watched as the power man walked from his pickup to the power pole that brought electricity to the distribution cabinet from which he had just fled. He raised his tree trimming pole to the power line and looked over at the utility building. Another electrical panel in the building had just exploded, scaring all of us once more. The big man quickly recovered and cut the line.

My eye went back to the utility building. The exploding electrical panels make a very noticeable noise when they blow up. This is joined by a percussion felt in your organs.

The next explosion was much different. Not only was the building made out of concrete block, it also had steel running from its foundation to the top of the walls every three feet. Each one of these cells was then filled with concrete. The building was truly a bunker.

This piece of structural engineering prevented large chunks of the walls from being launched through the windshield of my beloved command post, when a large explosion ripped through the building. The force of the explosion deposited the hazmat crew, standing over 100 feet away, right on their asses.

Lynn and I sat in stunned disbelief as the entire roof that once covered the good-sized building rocketed straight up into the sky. I estimate that the roof hit the zenith of its flight somewhere around 200 feet. Time seemed to freeze as the roof stopped heading toward the sun and hovered for a little while. Gravity took over and the roof did several revolutions before crashing to the ground. It was quite spectacular.

# Gut

I was pulled from my daze by a knocking at my window. It was power man. I rolled the window down, feeling vindicated over my near psychic ability to predict the future. He looked at me and said, "As you may have already noticed, the electrical to the complex has been secured."

# The Anatomy and Physiology of Leadership

## Backbone (Spine)

Backbone    181

# *The Anatomy and Physiology of Leadership*

*Backbone*

# The Anatomy and Physiology of Leadership

# Backbone (Spine)

## Basic Leadership Capability

The backbone is the major structural member for the body and gives us humanoids the basic capability to stand up straight and tall like our mom told us to do. Without our backbone, we would be unsupported blobs of various organs that would pretty much land and stay in one place. Perhaps without backbones, there would be little low-rise taxies that would scoop us up and hold our heads (up) as they hauled us around to show us what was cookin' in Blobsville.

Life is a lot more active and fun with a backbone, so we should all enjoy the elevated view and quietly thank the human design team every time we go out for a fly ball, or do the rhumba with Waldo or Chiquita. Our backbone also provides that same sort of stand up straight and tall leadership capability in the difficult situations that leaders will always encounter.

It's really pretty easy to do all the standard-issue leadership/boss stuff when everything is going good and the fan is blowing just nice, clean air. When the yucky stuff gets caught up in the blades and gets flung all over the landscape is when the clock really starts on authentic leadership.

In fact, during routine, good times, leaders generally don't learn a whole lot about the world, the human condition, or themselves. During these happy times, most of our workers really don't need much of our grand-exalted boss direction. They are mostly nice, smart, honest folks who typically show up to do a shift of good work, and then go home (during most routine times, the best thing bosses can do is to not screw with the workers so they can do their work).

# The Anatomy and Physiology of Leadership

## Backbone (cont.)

Tough times and situations are a lot different from routine times. They require effective leaders to make difficult decisions and then cause those decisions to come to life. Boss performance in tough spots many times involves unpopular, messy, painful stuff that becomes the definition of the structural stability and durability of the boss's backbone. Simply, tough times are showtime for effective bosses.

Backbone strength and durability is the result of lots of development stuff like good family values ("mom management"), positive organizational role models, and a strong effective internal culture. Increasing responsibility progressively builds "bone tissue" over a person's career. The actual operational experience (i.e., resistance, fights, road rash, and lots of tough lessons, etc.) that produces the battle scars will either assassinate the weak or develop smart, tough leaders.

Organizations which survive and prosper particularly during periods of active change (like now) are generally not nice, tidy, safe places to manage. Effective bosses must be willing to provide the vision, planning, and direction to break loose the organizational inertia required to jump into current windows of opportunity. Such redirection will always involve change agents getting scuffed up--from a little to a lot.

Like all other body parts, the capability of the backbone can be an enormous strength if it is balanced with other body parts (particularly the heart), or a painful weakness if it is unbalanced and overused by itself. Any idiot can be just tough (a thug).

Every job on every level of the organization requires its own special combination of supervision, management, and leadership. Consistently doing this combination is a tough challenge and requires backbone on the part of that person. Good bosses help workers provide their own combination of supervision/management/leadership.

# The Anatomy and Physiology of Leadership

## Backbone (cont.)

Sometimes each of us will fail to provide our own effective level of self-control and self-direction. When this happens, that person's boss must make up for what the worker has not provided for themselves. Simply, the boss must provide the parts of external control to make up for the lack of internal self-control that the worker did not do for themselves. Providing this "make up" is a huge boss job and can be extremely difficult. This becomes "showtime" for the boss and on that day becomes what that boss is actually paid to do.

Having a boss who effectively acts out "you do it for yourself, or I'll do it for you" defines the boss more than any other single thing. When this is required, all the boss talk must be connected into backbone-directed action. The trick is for effective bosses to use the strength and resolve of their backbone in quiet, positive, nice, constructive ways to move people and processes along in smart, sensible, and progressive directions. The most un-nice thing a boss can do is to accept substandard performance.

## Rules of Engagement

- Don't drop what you promised to carry.
- Only lift what you can carry (physically and emotionally).
- Carry your share of the weight.
- Stand up straight and tall/stand up for yourself.
- Send a consistent message about:
    - what you stand for
    - what you won't stand for.

# The Anatomy and Physiology of Leadership

## Backbone (cont.)

- Always try to balance equal parts of smart/nice/tough.

- Battle management:

  - Avoid fights (the best fight is the one you prevented).
  - Pick your fights.
  - If you must fight--win.
  - If you put someone in a corner... give them a door out.

- Tough times/situations:

  - Don't avoid tough stuff.
  - Try to control timing.
  - Do tough stuff smart.
  - Try not to create losers (if you hurt 'em, heal 'em)
  - Plan to both survive and recover.
  - Never give up.

- Use progressive resistance (sets/reps) to get stronger and use progressive lessons to get smarter.

- Front-end load positive organizational (and personal) performance with:

  - standard operating procedures
  - effective training
  - supported application (service delivery)
  - timely critique
  - ongoing revision.

## *The Anatomy and Physiology of Leadership*

# Backbone (Spine)

Not all heroes have backbone. Most heroes are manufactured in a span of a few seconds, generally after taking some type of action that most people would define as crazy or even suicidal. Rarer is the person who becomes a hero from the accumulated accomplishments over a long span of time. One is quick, fueled by a blast of courage (or momentary lapse of reason); the other requires hard work over a long haul, determination, and backbone.

I have worked alongside people who routinely performed tasks that people would describe as heroic. These individuals were not afraid of operating in the confines of a burning building. They had done it hundreds of times (even thousands), and most of them performed like it was just another day at the office.

The vast majority of these associates were spectacular human beings and would be offended that someone even suggested that they were heroic.

In a much smaller corner of our organization there existed a few tortured souls who did the same job, with the same level of bravery; yet they had the spine of a jellyfish. Backbone describes having strength of character and standing up for something you believe in. There is a big difference between taking physical risks and having backbone.

Backbone is not popular. The least popular person in the group is usually the one with the most backbone. It takes moral courage to go against the will (or popular opinion) of the masses. People who have no spine will always go along to get along. This social dynamic is true for any group of people.

Occupying the other end of the scale are the folks who have all of the backbone in the world, but they squander it on petty issues and half-baked hallucinations. When this mental disorder goes chronic, it leaves its victim seriously out of balance and generally out of gas. Backbone must be used in conjunction with the proper amounts of ego control, logic, and soul.

This is the story of two leaders, Alan Brunacini and Pat Cantelme. These two pioneers used their backbones to great effect, not only saving the organization they loved, but also creating an environment that caused it to flourish. It has all of the classic human elements--ego, power, cowardice, reconciliation, and steeled-toed shoes.

It had been three years since the Phoenix Fire Department had coronated its new Fire Chief--Big Al. The fire department underwent more change in that 36-month period, than it had in the fifty years that preceded it. The new chief was in his early forties, unusually

## The Anatomy and Physiology of Leadership

# Backbone (Spine)

young to lead an organization with almost 1,000 members, and the mission of protecting one of America's ten biggest cities. His twenty-year career was a grand plan in preparation for becoming the leader. He started at the bottom rung and worked his way up the ladder, serving in every line position. His last assignment was the number two man, running the Fire Fighting Division.

During the infancy of his career, he took an educational leave, moved his young family to Stillwater, Oklahoma, and earned a bachelor's degree from OSU in fire protection engineering. When he promoted to the officer ranks, he went to graduate school, earning a master's degree in public administration from Arizona State University.

He had grown up in an organization that was constricted and resistive to change. When Big Al took the helm, it was the dawn of a new era.

Pat Cantelme was destined to become a labor leader. He attended a catholic high school run by Franciscan monks, nuns, and for a little while, by Pat.

Cantelme was the student body president when he led a walkout and strike by the student body over the human right's issue of the song selection in the cafeteria's juke box.

The school's religious leaders decided to deal with their upstart rabble-rouser in the most benevolent manner, Pat was suspended from school and his parents were asked to find another educational institution for their young activist.

All things considered, he got off easy. A thousand years earlier this same group would have drawn and quartered him.

Pat was the Phoenix Fire Department's first 18-year old firefighter hire. A decade later, when Pat was elected the President of the Firefighter's Union, Local 493, all of the pieces were on the board and the game was underway.

Cantelme was young, intelligent, cared deeply about the fire department, and he had the determination and vision to make things better. Looking back on it, Pat Cantelme was the strongest driving force in turning the City of Phoenix into one of the premier workplace/employers that exists anywhere. There should be a statue of him in front of City Hall.

Throughout the 1970s, our local was at odds with the city over the issues concerning firefighter pay and benefits. The firefighter's union was seeking pay parody with the Phoenix Police. Firefighters worked longer hours and made less money. The city

# The Anatomy and Physiology of Leadership

countered that firefighters had too much free time between fires and didn't work as hard as the hometown-crime fighters.

The city was playing with the idea of having on-duty fire companies empty money out of parking meters. The disagreement between the two sides was turning nasty.

The city's new fire chief added another dimension to the mix by going into the emergency medical business and implementing a comprehensive set of SOPs (or rules) for conducting fire fighting operations. These changes more than quadrupled the fire department's work load.

I was hired in 1980. A week before my academy class graduated, our two training captains informed us that the union was taking a strike vote that evening. We all drove home that night contemplating our uncertain future. Cooler heads prevailed and the strike (which would have been an unmitigated disaster) was defeated. This still didn't change the fact that both sides didn't get along.

While our union and their masters in city hall went about the business of playing out the standard roles in their dysfunctional relationship, the fire chief continued his march toward improving firefighter safety and service delivery to the community. This created an atmosphere where the members were doing more work, change was coming at them at the speed of light, and they had the feeling that the city fathers ultimately didn't care about them. These feelings of resentment were bleeding into the closed confines of our organization. As fate would have it, the insignificant and petty issue of shoe selection would be our crossroads.

Chief Brunacini made the observation that firefighters routinely found themselves walking, standing, and working in places that were hazardous to their feet. Many firefighters wore black athletic shoes, as a standard piece of their daily uniform. Somehow the fire chief made the connection that tenny-runners weren't the most appropriate, safety-oriented occupational footwear choice for the emergency scene.

This piece of information got passed onto our department's uniform committee, which was made up of representatives from labor (firefighters) and management (chiefs). They were charged with approving several different types of safety shoes that firefighters could wear as part of their regular uniform.

Like most committees, they fought for months about something so stupid as shoe versus boot versus stiletto heel. All they had to do was

## The Anatomy and Physiology of Leadership

# Backbone (Spine)

approve any black safety shoe that had been certified by ANSI or OSHA or any of the other national organizations that approve safety gear.

It is a commonly held belief that a group is always more effective than a single individual. If you believe this, then it is also true that a group can be more bullheaded and stupid than a single individual.

The deadline for choosing shoes had come and gone. This didn't stop the fire chief from asking the simple question, "What safety shoes did you guys approve for the work force?"

The committee spouted some mumbo-jumbo that reaffirmed their ineffectiveness in making simple decisions. The fire chief patiently listened and then replied, "Fine, we are going to wear a three-quarter length, lace up, chukka style boot. Have a nice day."

The fire chief's shoe choice also came with an implementation plan, complete with requirement date that fell several weeks after we received our yearly uniform allowance. The shoe plight was nearing its one-year anniversary.

In a day and age where everyone was losing their minds over negotiating in good faith, binding arbitration, and mutual respect, one would think something as mundane as wearing a safety shoe would go almost unnoticed. Wrong. The shoe became the line in the sand. The more emotional members (many of them union officials) used the shoe as a war cry and rallying point--"If the city won't treat us as equals, then we don't have to wear the fire chief's stupid shoe."

As the deadline approached, the issue took on a life of its own, and the steel-toed shoe became known as the "Bruno Boot."

I had been temporarily assigned to a downtown, multi-company firehouse. This station was staffed with very vocal labor activists. None of them planned on wearing the fire department's latest foot fashion.

They were young, full of vim and vigor, and seemed to be happiest when they had an issue they could be angry about together. They were also decent people and never gave me any grief about wearing the new shoes. I purchased the shoes when I was hired as a new firefighter, and the issue held no emotion for me. They were pissed off but nice enough to know the difference between the fire chief and my father.

The only unexpressed opinion was owned by one of the captains assigned to the station. He fancied himself as being urbane and highly intelligent. He gave off the air that he was a

# The Anatomy and Physiology of Leadership

little smarter and better than the rest of us. There was no way he was coming out of the closet over his secret lust that the fire chief put his troops in the new boot.

When the topic of shoes came up, Captain Creamed Corn would remain silent, leave the room or change the subject. His favorite topic to rant about was the incompetence of anyone and everyone who had less than twenty years on the job.

Years later, I learned that Captain Cosmopolitan regularly phoned the fire chief during those tumultuous days to let him know he supported his decision in requiring everyone to be safer.

These phone calls always took place on Captain Spineless's day off and when the fire chief was at home. It would be horrible if the group found out that Captain Jellyfish took a stand that differed from the rest of the throng.

Several days before the big shoe showdown, our meek captain phoned Big Al to offer some final words of encouragement. This issue had polarized the fire department and come Monday you were going to pledge allegiance with the shoes you showed up to work in. The fire chief asked Captain Anonymous how he planned on riding the fence and remaining neutral on the big day.

"Well Alan, that's easy. I took vacation on Monday."

In the end, Captain No Show wasn't part of anything.

The days leading up to the deadline were punctuated and filled with chest beating and threats. Seeing a disaster on the horizon, a few days before the big showdown, the fire chief and union president had a quiet get together at a local greasy spoon.

The two of them came to the conclusion that they really liked and respected each other. The shoe problem was the symptom of a much larger issue in which both of them were caught. They had come to the same conclusion--their organization couldn't go where they wanted to take it, if the two of them spent all day fighting with one another.

What they did next was really simple and went completely counter to the course of action that powerful individuals usually take when they are challenged. They both gave in a little.

The fire chief postponed the showdown at the OK Corral and the union president made the proclamation that everyone was going to wear the new manly footwear.

# The Anatomy and Physiology of Leadership

## Backbone (Spine)

The two leaders agreed to share power. Their alliance became the template for the entire organization.

The fire department quickly became a place that was operated (functionally) by needs and objectives, replacing the traditional (ego driven) rank-based paramilitary model.

This new approach didn't eliminate disagreement, it simply gave us a productive way to resolve issues, without tearing the group apart.

Our efforts were focused on finding the common ground, then moving in the direction of refining the way we operated as a fire department. This provided a system where people could spend their time doing what they did best.

This revolution couldn't have taken place if the fire chief and union president hadn't checked their egos at the door. Both men had the backbone to put their differences aside and do what was best for the organization, the public that it served, and in the end for themselves.

With their direction, guidance, patience, and leadership, the Phoenix Fire Department became one of the world's great organizations. It's ironic that when our two leaders gave their power away to one another, they ended up becoming the most powerful and respected people in their fields.

# The Anatomy and Physiology of Leadership

## Funny Bone

# The Anatomy and Physiology of Leadership

*Funny Bone*

# The Anatomy and Physiology of Leadership

# Funny Bone

## Basic Leadership Capability

The funny bone is the location of the leader/boss's most important human sense--their sense of humor. We can lose any (or all) of our other capabilities and senses and still survive. But, if we lose our sense of humor, it's all over, curtains, the end, ugghh. Life is simply too cold, cruel, and difficult to absorb up close and personally without humor. Funny business gives us the absolutely essential capability to take what we are doing seriously, without taking ourselves the same way.

It's pretty easy for bosses to begin to believe in their own inherent, dazzling beautifulness, and look in the mirror and see superman/wonderwoman smile back at them.

In reality, most of us really look pretty silly a lot of the time; so we might as well learn to laugh at ourselves along with everyone else.

The basic output of the funny bone is to create laughter and fun. This is why it is such an important body part-- without laughter and fun we might as well be a rock, a chair, a toaster, or some other slug-like object. Laughter brings people together and creates the capability to stand back from a difficult situation for a moment and effectively refocus. Laughter also produces squads of angels dressed up as endorphins (pleasure hormones) that rush to critical places in our body during tough times to body slam stress demons that are trying to wreck those body parts.

Scientific studies have recently discovered that inside our funny bone humor center, there are continuous Marx Brothers and Three Stooges movies showing--these movies give us an ongoing, standby humor capability. During tough times, it's pretty easy to

# The Anatomy and Physiology of Leadership

## Funny Bone (cont.)

"click" them on and watch a little nonsense for a minute or two... all the scowling grumps will wonder where the twinkle in your eye came from (a big negotiating advantage).

The funny bone is our only portable body part. It has the special capability to move around the body and connect with all the other pieces and parts to create the humor and fun that goes with (and complements) that component. How (and why) the funny bone attaches to a particular body part is regulated by each person's personality.

Some people's humor emerges from their brain--they sort of naturally think up funny stuff. Others are emotionally funny--their funny bone attaches to their heart. Others use their facial expression or body language to create humor. It becomes a major skill for the funny bone to develop the versatility to connect with each individual and use a special combination of that person's body parts.

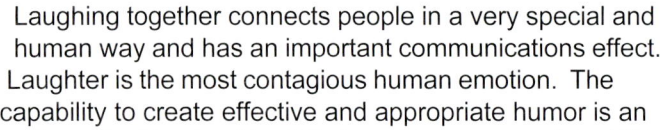

Laughing together connects people in a very special and human way and has an important communications effect. Laughter is the most contagious human emotion. The capability to create effective and appropriate humor is an important leadership skill. Smart bosses use this skill to connect with others, and this connection becomes the foundation for effective two-way communication. Simply, laughing together encourages talking and listening together. A laughing boss, who is sharing a funny thing, creates a happy moment in the relationship.

A happy team is generally a more productive team and is always a healthier one. With self-directed humor the boss sends a message that they are human, not perfect, and approachable. People laughing together creates a pleasant sound and causes

# The Anatomy and Physiology of Leadership

## Funny Bone (cont.)

the laughees to open up and become more receptive to each other.

Kids must become the laughter/fun models for grown-ups. Little, beginning people aren't screwed up with a lot of serious junk that rains on their funny-bone parade. To them, everything is funny and they can have fun for thirty minutes with a rubber band and a paper clip (little kids laugh over 400 times a day--adults only 30... growing up sucks). Given that we can't get the little twerps to go to work and make the mortgage payment while we stay home and play, we had better let our funny bone loose and enjoy the ride.

### Rules of Engagement

- Look for humor in routine situations.

- Use humor to reduce tension and stress.

- Use humor to move forward and strengthen situations, resolution, and relationships.

- Whenever possible, direct humor to the "big people."

- When you tease yourself:

  - You look human (unstuff your shirt).
  - Others relax and open up.
  - You are continually amused.

- Laughing leads to listening (remember basic reality of education: That which is learned without mirth is forgotten without regret).

# The Anatomy and Physiology of Leadership

## Funny Bone (cont.)

- Avoid humor that hurts:

  - Don't beat up the "little guy."
  - Don't kick people when they're down.
  - Don't hurt people's feelings.
  - Mean is never funny.

- Use humor that is politically sensible and correct/avoid illegal sexist/racist humor.

- It ain't fun (or funny) unless it's fun for everyone.

- Study people who use funny stuff effectively--pay attention to words, phrases, gestures, timing, and delivery.

- Take yourself lightly, let go, and laugh lots.

## The Anatomy and Physiology of Leadership

# Funny Bone

One of the things that separates us from our ancestors is our more highly developed sense of humor. Looking back as recently as the early 1900s, most of the photographic records reflect stern, constipated expressions on the people's faces. Go back a few decades earlier, and it appears that right before the photographer snapped the picture, he gut shot his subjects. Compare this to today, where everyone in the frame is all smiles.

I believe we have matured as a species by developing our sense of humor and giving ourselves permission to enjoy life. After all, what is the purpose of living the life of Ebenezer Scrooge, when you can accomplish the same set of things and have fun while doing it? It's really a no-brainer, and the choice is all yours--you can decide to be happy, or you can choose to be miserable. There is no need for each of us to dig up the bones of the dead in order to beat ourselves. Life will throw enough rotting carcasses in our direction.

One of the main sources of frustration in many peoples' daily lives comes from their bosses. This funny-bone tale revolves around the relationship between a worker and a boss. It is not your typical subordinate/supervisor story, because there is nothing typical about the characters. They both occupy opposite ends of the spectrum.

Laurence (not Larry) was a senior member of the Phoenix Fire Department. He was promoted to captain a couple years before the US entered the Vietnam War. Laurence possessed an incompetence that bordered on genius. There are stories surrounding him that will live forever in the popular culture of the Phoenix Fire Department. Many of our youngest generation of firefighters have never met the man because he retired years ago, but the fact that they know many of the details of his illustrious career speaks volumes about his management and leadership abilities and the mark he left on our organization.

A wise man once told me you should learn something from everyone you encounter. He said that most people make the mistake that you can't learn anything from the mean, inept, crazy, and addicted. It was his feeling that learning what to avoid, and how not to be, was every bit as important as learning the positive human qualities. One of his favorite sayings was, "You must know sin to fight sin." Laurence was a shining example of how not to be.

One of the earliest Laurence stories is based on a three-gallon galvanized bucket.

Laurence was backing a fire engine into the apparatus bay when he inadvertently backed over and flattened a bucket. Laurence

*Funny Bone*

# The Anatomy and Physiology of Leadership

## Funny Bone

parked the truck, noticed the bucket he just killed, and looked around for any potential witnesses. Seeing none, he collected the bucket and deposited it underneath some trash in the dumpster behind the station.

Unbeknownst to Laurence, one of the members of the crew observed the entire event and retrieved the squashed bucket from the trash bin.

For the next five years, this bucket followed Laurence everywhere. He found it in his locker, the front seat of the rig, his personal car, his dormitory bed, and finally in the shed behind his house. I'm sure it visited him in his dreams, and it will litter the white light he sees, when his life finally comes to an end. Firefighters have highly developed funny bones.

Laurence had been removed from several of the stations he was assigned to during the last half of his career, as the result of the disciplinary process. His tenure at the airport was cut short when Laurence ordered the engineer whom he was supervising to drive the crash rescue truck across an active runway.

His new assignment was on a busy inner-city paramedic engine company. That gig ended when the oncoming shift found the reserve rig that Captain Laurence and his crew switched into (because their regular engine developed pump problems on an early morning car fire) had little to no equipment on it. This led to a lengthy discipline festival for the entire crew and a staff assignment for Captain Laurence.

One of Laurence's last assignments, prior to his much celebrated retirement, was at a single engine company firehouse in south Phoenix. This fire station was housed in a double-wide mobile home, set in the middle of cotton fields.

The most extraordinary thing in the entire first-due area was Steve, the engineer who drove the rig. It was a marriage made in dream land--Laurence was the king of ineptitude; Steve was the prince of practical jokes.

For the fifteen years that Steve worked for the fire department, he was either the architect or a major principle in most of the unauthorized department-wide high jinks that went on. He was always pursuing the latest get-rich quick scheme--gold mines, pyramid schemes, Amway, penny stocks, and Cabbage Patch Dolls to name but a few. Easy money was Steve's pastime, but his bread and butter was the antic.

# The Anatomy and Physiology of Leadership

Many of the previous firefighters assigned to Captain Laurence dreaded coming to work. Steve had a different philosophy; he delighted in the opportunities it provided him.

Before Steve began employment with the Phoenix Fire Department he had a couple years' stint with a minor league baseball team. Steve was athletically gifted and had the lean, hard physique of a shortstop. He could throw the ball a mile and hit it over the fence. The thing that kept him from the major leagues was his lack of concentration and focus. He played outfield, and on more than one occasion missed entire innings of defensive play because he was having conversations with the spectators. This became well known with opposing teams, and their batters would hit the ball towards Steve on the good chance that he was chatting it up with the fans. With each new catchable fly ball that turned into a hit, Steve's baseball career drew to a close.

Right around the time Steve graduated from our training academy, an incident occurred that cemented his reputation. There are a dozen or so smaller cities that border the western edge of Phoenix. Each one of them has its own fire department. Steve spent a few months working as a reserve for one of these departments during the time between his failed baseball career and his employment with Phoenix.

One day, some misguided individual began calling people who resided in one of these cities. This lunatic represented himself as a high-ranking official with the state's largest electrical utility. We were a month or so into the summer, a time when most desert dwellers covet and rely on an uninterrupted supply of power.

The imposter told the unsuspecting homeowners that the entire western power grid was going to be shut down for maintenance for at least three to four days, and they needed to take all of their perishables to a local fire station where they would be assigned their own private cold storage unit. The caller then instructed the homeowner to call ten friends and provide them with the same information and in turn to have them call ten of their friends.

That night on the news, there was a story about panic in the west valley where a local firehouse was mobbed by hundreds of people who had shown up with enough food to feed most third-world nations. They were demanding access to the refrigerators that the electric company had promised them.

*Funny Bone*

## The Anatomy and Physiology of Leadership

# Funny Bone

The reporter interviewed the genuine high-ranking guy in charge of the utility company, who talked straight into the camera and swore that there were absolutely no plans to shut the western power grid down for any reason. He also vowed to find the madman behind this prank and prosecute him to the full extent of the law.

Several weeks later, the phone company had figured out that over a dozen calls had been made from Steve's home phone in the minutes that led up to the fake power outage panic. Later on that day, Steve told the assemblage of police officers that he had been doing yard work on the day in question and had taken his phone outside so he wouldn't miss any important phone calls. After he finished with his outside chores, he went in and cleaned up, completely forgetting his phone outside for the remainder of the day and that evening.

No one had been hurt or damaged in anyway, and Steve's story added enough confusion to the situation where the police dropped the matter with a stern lecture about leaving one's phone outside where any misguided moron could access it and cause a small-scale panic. Within minutes everyone on the Phoenix Fire Department knew who Steve was.

Every Friday the fire department distributes an internal communications tool called the "buckslip." This is a series of memos, available assignments (open spots on engine and ladder companies), procedure changes, current events, a question answer section, and a classified section (primarily used by firefighters who are getting divorced and liquidating their assets).

Steve forged a memo and stapled it into their station's weekly buckslip. The memo said that since the fire department had added so many new procedures and guidelines for improving the way we handle emergency incidents, it had caused a certain level of confusion regarding the correct way to do things. To help crews in the field cope with these changes, management decided to install a library on all engine companies. During that period of time, engine companies had split supply line hose beds. Each bed carried 500 feet of 3 ½" hose.

The memo went on to say that a 6-foot tall filing cabinet had been delivered to each station and was to be filled with a variety of operational manuals and other reference materials. The left supply line hose bed was to be emptied so the filling cabinet could be installed, along with a full-sized desk and office chair.

# The Anatomy and Physiology of Leadership

It was Captain Laurence's first shift with Steve, and he bought the fake memo hook, line, and sinker.

Laurence and the probationary firefighter had unloaded the left hose bed. Captain Larry went into the station to get Steve and the senior firefighter to assist with setting up the mobile office. The senior firefighter was a twenty-five year veteran and he was fully aware of Steve's reputation. When he went outside and saw the pile of hose, he asked his captain why he had dumped a perfectly good hose bed. Larry showed him the memo in the buckslip. Before the senior firefighter finished reading the memo, he knew it was one of Steve's ruses.

He said, "Come on Skip, don't tell me you believe this bullshit. This is too stupid to be real. You know this has Steve written all over it."

Captain Larry wasn't buying it. The senior firefighter had to call their chief and have him tell his brainiac captain that the memo was a fake. Steve swore he had nothing to do with it.

Over the next few months, Steve continued his mischievous ways. Steve had placed a wiring harness out of an old dump truck under the dash of their engine company. Later in the day they were responding code three, and while Steve was driving, he bent down and grabbed a handful of wires from under the dash and pulled them out. He shook the wires at Captain Larry and told him they were causing the truck's diesel engine to lose power and hurting their fuel economy. He then threw the mass of brightly colored wires out the window. Captain Larry sat in stunned amazement as the truck seemed to gain power and blow less black smoke from its exhaust pipe. Captain Larry was starting to believe that Steve was a genius.

Their working relationship continued this way for the better part of a year. Steve had Captain Larry convinced that the station was possessed. Captain Larry was certain that raw sewage was somehow finding its way into their water. The city water department was called out on numerous occasions. Each time they would explain that it was physically impossible for this to happen, at worst it was dirt in the line caused by a fractured water main somewhere. Captain Larry would always identify this problem occurring in the shower.

It seemed that every time he showered, brown water came out of the shower head. It was never a fractured water line; Steve would unscrew the shower head from the pipe and load it up with chicken bullion cubes.

*Funny Bone*

# The Anatomy and Physiology of Leadership

## Funny Bone

Captain Larry was looking to get out of his current station before he was ever sent there. He had done his time, put in for and received another assignment, and now was spending his final week amidst the tall cotton. The crew was sitting around the table, drinking coffee, and reading the paper one morning when Steve came across an article that he shared with his comrades.

The Acme Company had put in a recall for a certain blow dryer they sold. It was determined that this particular model had an asbestos lining that would eventually flake off, blowing fine particles of the cancer-causing material into one's wet hair.

It appeared to Captain Larry that the water department had finally fixed the sewage problem, and he had started showering at the station again. That evening he went through his hygiene ritual, which included scrubbing his face with some type of abrasive powder. After drying off, he plugged in his trusty Acme blow dryer, held it to his head like a gun, hit the on button, and disappeared in a cloud of cornstarch.

Captain Larry came out of the fog of the bathroom choking. He had white powder caked in his hair and plastered into his overgrown eyebrows. After Captain Larry took another shower, Steve gave him the number to a top-notch attorney. The Acme Company would not get away with this.

Their relationship was well known throughout the organization. Neither one of them ever said anything negative about the other. Steve thought Captain Larry was a nice enough guy and easy to get along with. So what that he was clueless. The crew packed him when they needed to, and he never gave them any grief. Captain Larry idolized Steve. He came to think that Steve was wasting his life on the fire department and should go back to school to become a rocket scientist. In some strange way they both came to need and love one another.